The Dinkum Aussie Dunny Companion

The Dinkum Aussie Dunny Companion

Nicholas Reed

MaxiBooks

MaxiBooks is an imprint of Maximedia (Pty) Ltd
(A.C.N. 002 666 579)
PO Box 529
Kiama NSW 2533
Australia

ISBN 1 875 666 01 X

1098765432

Cover design by **Look Serious Design, Sydney.**

Wholly designed, typeset and printed in Australia.

CONTENTS

Brain teasers

Short stories

Become a professor of useless info!

LIKE it or not – you can't escape the dunny. In fact, statisticians say each of us graces it with our presence around 11 minutes and 30 seconds *EVERY SINGLE DAY* – which tallies up to about *HALF A WEEK A YEAR or SEVERAL MONTHS* of your life!

Are you letting all that valuable time go to waste? No longer – thanks to THE DINKUM AUSSIE DUNNY COMPANION. It's the first book designed to let your enforced visits to the dunny enrich your mind – and have loads of fun at the same time!

Flick through quickly and you'll see what we mean ... whether you're on the dunny for a few seconds or a few minutes, there's something of interest in this book for you – from tantalising trivia to quizzes, gags, cartoons, brain teasers and classic all-Australian tales.

In fact, it's packed with enough of the funny, the weird and the wonderful to drive you potty – or to make you a **Bachelor of Useless Info**. Which is exactly what you can become – just turn to Page 129 and find out how to get your own **PERSONALISED CERTIFICATE** awarding you just that title to hang behind your dunny door.

Even having fun should have its rewards – and what better way to become a Bachelor of Useless Info than on the dunny!

SHADY CHARACTERS

How to play: Unscramble these five Australian rivers to fit into the grid. When you have solved the puzzle, the shaded letters will spell out a sixth

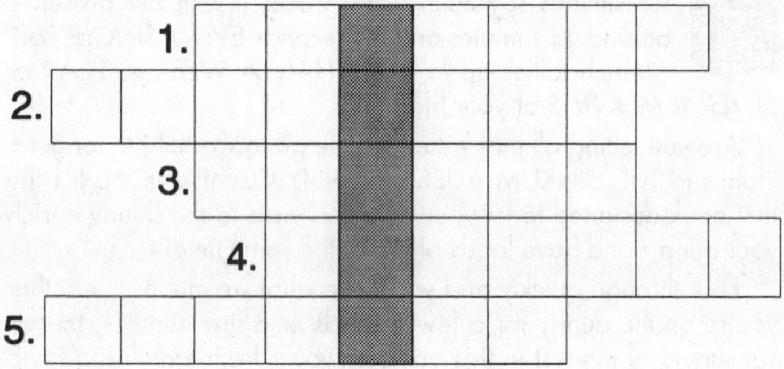

Clues

1. **GINLARD**
2. **RIOAVCIT**
3. **PANNEE**
4. **REOGGES**
5. **ZYTFOIR**

Answers on Page 190

Strange, strange ... but TRUE

AN inheritance of close on $100,000 awaits anyone who can satisfy the Public Trustee Office in London that he is Jesus Christ. An eccentric man named Ernest Digweed bequeathed the money in 1977 to "the Son of God" to finance Him during the Second Coming. About 30 people have unsuccessfully tried to claim the money so far.

Who tonight, Eugenie?

French Emperor Louis Napoleon had a most accommodating wife last century – Eugenie regularly rounded up prostitutes for his use and even bathed them to make sure they were clean enough for her husband. But once in bed with the Emperor, it was not a case of anything goes – the women were prohibited from ever touching the Imperial **face**.

Mahatma Gandhi, on the other hand, was the world's weirdest celibate – he regularly slept with naked women to prove to himself he could not be tempted.

Pet(ty) Points!

Squids are difficult to keep as pets – in captivity they often commit suicide by eating their own tentacles.

Dog lover and poet Lord Byron kept a bear as a pet while a student at Cambridge – because dogs were prohibited in students' rooms.

Bloody oath!

Count Dracula actually existed – and the monster by that name who lived in present-day Romania during the 15th Century was even more bloodthirsty than his vampire counterpart. Nicknamed "Vlad the Impaler", he loved locking people inside buildings which were then set alight.

'THAT'S ONE OF THE DRAWBACKS OF BUTTERFLY HUNTING IN TRANSALVAINIA !!

???????

Probably the briefest correspondence ever conducted was between French author Victor Hugo and his publisher. After sending the manuscript of *Les Miserables* to the publisher, Hugo followed up with a letter reading only: "?". The reply? "!"

Leonardo da Vinci, on the other hand, could write with one hand at the same time he was using the other to sketch or paint. American President James Garfield, while no artist, could simultaneously write Greek with one hand and Latin with the other.

Not a girl's best friend

Do you doubt that opals are unlucky? Then wait till you've read the amazing experience of King Alphonso II of Spain. His wedding gift to his wife was an opal ring – and within days of putting it on, she was dead. Alphonso lent the ring to his sister to wear at the funeral – and soon she, too, was dead. Next was his sister-in-law, who perished three months after receiving the ring. The king, determined to prove it was all a coincidence, put on the ring himself – and died within a short time. To prevent it killing again, the ring was then hung around the neck of the statue of the Virgin of Almudena in Madrid.

And while on the subject of oddball jewellery: In a quest to relieve jaded jetsetters of their money, an American firm called Dino Drops Inc in 1969 introduced cufflinks made of petrified dinosaur dung. In parts of Italy, preserved squid eyes are strung and worn as bracelets and necklaces.

Almost certainly the largest ruby in the world was once owned by the King of the island of Ceylon. Marco Polo described it as "a span (around 23cm) long, as thick as a man's arm, and without a

STOP PRESS!

The second theme is again presented in dialogue fashion. The development and recapitulation are full of fresh ornamentation. There is the usual pause for the *cadenza*. Mozart has apparently left no records of what he and his sister did, apart from the final shake. The cadenzas usually used in this concerto are by Reinecke (1824—1910).

AND THE PILLOW ...

Patients responded in a positive manner. The staff are so enthusiastic I expect to eventually have them on every bed.

D.J. Williams, Director of Nursing, Belgrave Nursing

FINED £25

After admitting hating unlawful sexual intercourse with a girl under the age of 16 on a day unknown between August 31, 1964, and March 1 this year.

At Birkenhead, Ralph ... aged 18, a cleaner,

Listen with Mother, which this week offers the following short stories: The Tiny Wee Potato, Three Little Bicycles, Three Little Bicycles Go To Town, Three Little Bicycles Go to Sea, and something called The Great Big Red Thing for those who like a surprise

less skin — renamed Manix for Europe — is 3/100ths of a millimetre thick. Mr Degan says it is undetectable to the wearer.

"I've been in condoms for 27 years," the bustling entrepreneur says.

"I am going to make a fortune with Manix. Until now condoms on

... servants.

Mr. J. A. Dunn (Lab. Kirkdale) said M.P.s like himself with a wife, four children and no other income could now concentrate on Parliamentary beauties without financial worry.

He felt that M.P.s who

according to wildlife experts.

Crocodiles have been known to eat humans, but they are not regarded as maneaters.

flaw". The famous 13th Century explorer records that Kublai Khan unsuccessfully offered the treasures of an entire city in exchange for it.

Tipping the scales

How much does a human soul weigh? Intrigued by this question, a Swedish doctor spent years weighing patients on their deathbeds and in the mortuary. He concluded that on average the soul weighs 21 grams.

The earth, meanwhile, increases in weight by about 12 tonnes a day – from newly arrived meteorites.

Facts that hold water

To qualify as a shepherd in the Landes district of France, you must be able to herd sheep while perched on a pair of stilts. The unusual practice arose because much of the region is waterlogged, which slowed down ordinary pedestrian shepherds so much that they could not keep up with their flocks. The shepherds use a long walking stick to retain their balance in rough areas. In addition to keeping track of their sheep, the men also keep their feet dry.

To fill a Texas "ten-gallon" hat you need only three-quarters of a gallon of water. A jellyfish consists 95.4 per cent of water, while the water content of an adult human is between 58 and 66 per cent of body weight.

A load of hot air?

How you sound is determined by the air you breathe. Experiments have shown that if a person switched from fresh air (or what passes for it in modern cities) to helium, the gas causes the vocal cords to

FIND THE CELEBRITY

How to play

Starting with the circled letter, move one square at a time, in any direction, to find the hidden celebrity. All squares must be entered once only.

O	V	I	H
I	L	O	N
A	W	T	J
E	N	N	O

Answers on Page 190

contract so much that a bass voice changes to a soprano.

While on the subject: each year an adult breathes in around 4.45 million litres of air. The oxygen is distributed via 96,000 kilometres of blood vessels, some so thin that blood corpuscles can only pass through in single file. And if you think we're all flesh and blood, you've forgotten about the human body's 206 bones.

Who's counting?

Although the Milky Way alone contains around 100,000 million stars, on a clear night you can see no more than about 2500 stars with the naked eye.

At least 10 million people around the world celebrate their birthdays on the same day as you.

The wingspan of a modern Boeing 747 jumbo is longer than the 36.5 metres flown by the Wright Brothers during their famous first flight in December 1903.

March of Time

New Year's Day has not always been celebrated on January 1 The Romans started their year on March 25, and this was adopted throughout their Empire. When Pope Gregory III introduced a new calendar in 1582, Catholic countries changed to January 1, but Protestant nations did not. Scotland only accepted the new New Year in 1600, and England in 1752.

Strike a light!

Next time you turn on the electric light, spare a thought for poor Thomas Edison who spent years trying out more than 6000 different materials before deciding on a charred length of sewing thread as the ideal filament for his light bulb. Among others he tried out hair from his assistant's head, a blade of grass and fishline.

Potty patents

A musical potty, patented in 1957, played a tune when urinated into. Boots with pockets were patented in 1860 – for use by nudists! And while on the subject: Getting lost in the nude is not difficult at Warmbaths, South Africa, which boats the world's largest nudest resort. Known as the Beau Valley Country Club, it covers 400ha and caters for more than 20,000 nudists a year. The world's oldest operating nudest resort, at Klingsberg in West Germany, was established in 1903.

"A FANCY DRESS BALL! – MY GOD, FENSHAW, YOU'LL DO ANYTHING TO GET SOME CLOTHES ON!"

Sport spots

The hallmark of the modern Olympics is its amateurism, but amazingly top athletes competing in the original Greek Olympics were paid wages to allow them to train and compete full-time. They were also rewarded with money prizes.

America's first Sexual Olympics started in New York on 19 May 1978– and only ended forty-eight hours later. The winner was an Italian Romeo named Joe "The Pole" Scarlatti, who received a gold sceptre shaped like a phallus and $4800 for making love to twenty-seven women in four-and-a-half hours.

When streaking was fashionable some years ago, the Kenyan Government announced that any foreigner doing it would be deported.

Only in Australia

Australia's only "calendar house" is Mona Vale, near Ross in Tasmania's midlands. The three-storey Victorian Italianate mansion has 365 windows, 52 rooms, 12 chimneys, and seven entrances– representing days, weeks and months of the year. It was built between 1865 and 1869.

Xanthippe in WA is the only place in Australia with a name starting with the letter X. It was named by a scholarly settler after the bad-tempered wife of the Athenian philosopher Socrates. Whether the name-giver was having a dig at his own wife we will never know.

If you're looking for a lucky spot to place a bet, why not try ***Tarcoola****, on the South Australian fringe of the Nullarbor Plain. It was named after the winner of the 1893 Melbourne Cup.*

Sports Quiz

1 In his last international innings, during the Fifth Test against England at The Oval, Sir Donald Bradman scored (a) 210 not out; (b) a duck; (c) 55; (d) a century.

2 Australia's first - and only - Olympic gold medal for rugby football was won at the 1908 Games in (a) Athens; (b) Los Angeles; (c) London; (d) Vancouver.

3 The oldest existing road cycling race in the world covers 259.1km and has been held annually since 1895 between Melbourne and (a) Warrnambool; (b) Wangaratta; (c) Horsham; (d) Echuca.

4 The maiden name of former Australian world squash champion Heather McKay was (a) Charlton; (b) Court; (c) Blundell; (d) Grace.

5 The first horse to win the Melbourne and Caulfield Cups in the same year was (a) Phar Lap; (b) Carbine; (c) Poseidon; (d) Black Knight.

6 The largest sporting crowd in Australian history - 121,696 people - passed through the turnstiles to see the 1970 Australian Rules Grand Final in which Carlton beat (a) Footscray; (b) Essendon; (c) Collingwood; (d) Richmond.

7 The world's oldest lawn bowling club was formed in May 1880 in (a) Tasmania; (b) NSW; (c) Victoria; (d) Western Australia.

8 Jimmy Carruthers retained his world bantamweight boxing title in 1953 when he beat American Henry Gault in (a) Melbourne; (b) Geelong; (c) Brisbane; (d) Sydney.

9 The Claxton Shield has been awarded annually since 1931 to the champion State in (a) polo; (b) tennis; (c) baseball; (d) basketball.

10 The nickname of Australian swimmer Andrew Charlton, winner of a gold medal in the 1500 metres at the 1924 Paris Olympics, was (a) Speedy; (b) Fish; (c) Bonza; (d) Boy.

11 The first Australian to win the women's singles at Wimbledon, in 1963, was (a) Margaret Court; (b) Evonne Cawley; (c) Lesley Turner; (d) Wendy Turnbull.

12 The 9.1 metre Bermuda cutter that won the first Sydney-Hobart yacht race, which started on Boxing Day 1945, was the (a) Gypsey II; (b) Admiral Benbow; (c) Atlantis; (d) Rani.

13 The captain of the English team during the controversial "bodyline" tour of Australia in 1932-33 was (a) F.R. Spofforth; (b) Harold Larwood; (c) D.R. Jardine; (d) W.M. Woodfull.

14 Australia's first Olympic Gold Medalist was runner Edwin Flack, who won both the 800 metres and 1500 metres events in 1896 in (a) Rome; (b) Athens; (c) Paris; (d) London.

15 Peerless Fox won the first Adelaide Cup, run over a distance of 3200 metres, in (a) 1896; (b) 1922; (c) 1941; (d) 1951.

16 Les Darcy, Australia's middleweight and heavyweight boxing champion, was mourned by 100,000 people who filed past his coffin in Sydney in 1917 after he died at the age of 21 in (a) Britain; (b) the USA; (c) France; (d) Queensland.

17 The first Australian woman to win a place in an Olympic event - third in the 80 metres hurdles, 100 metres, and 400 metres relay at the 1948 London Games - was (a) Shirley Strickland; (b) Marjorie Jackson; (c) Winsome Cripps; (d) Betty Cuthbert.

18 The first Australian cricketer to score a century before lunch in a Test - at Manchester in 1902 - was (a) Don Bradman; (b) Victor Trumper; (c) Clem Hill; (d) Charlie Macartney.

19 The Federation Cup, first won by Australia in 1964, is an international competition for women in (a) golf; (b) softball; (c) squash; (d) tennis.

20 The game first introduced into Australia in 1875 by army officers from India, in which chukkers are an important feature, is (a) baseball; (b) archery; (c) polo; (d) lacrosse.

Answers on Page 190

CHANGE-A-WORD

How to play

By altering one letter at a time, can you, in four moves, turn "FLIPS"into "COINS".A proper word must be formed at each change.

F	L	I	P	S
C	O	I	N	S

Answers on Page 190

Crime and (severe) punishment

TARRING and feathering as a punishment became part of English law in 1189 during the reign of King Richard I (Richard the Lion Heart). The Act stipulated that a robber found on board a ship sailing to the crusades "shall first be shaved, then boiling pitch shall be poured on his head, and a cushion of feathers shook over it".

Treason, too, was a hazardous occupation, particularly in 17th Century England. The sentence passed on one, named Walcot, in 1696 ordered that he be "hanged by the neck and dropped to the ground alive and that his private parts be cut off and that his bowels within his belly be taken and put upon a fire and burned while he lives and that his head be cut off and that his body be divided into four parts to be placed where it may please His Majesty the King to assign them".

Royal roulette?

King Henry VIII, whose lust for women led to the founding of the Church of England, insisted that his male staff should be punished if they indulged in extra-marital sex. The regulations for his Officers of the Bedchamber stated: "Such pages as cause the maids of the King's household to become mothers will go without beer for a month."

What an ordeal!

The word ordeal in Old English literally meant judgment – because it was used to determine guilt or innocence. The form of ordeal depended on the accused person's station in life or the nature of the crime. In ordeal by fire, high-ranking persons had to walk blind-folded and in bare feet over red-hot plough shares. If the accused showed no wounds after three days, he was judged innocent. Common people had to endure ordeal by water: a hand was plunged into boiling water and any injury was considered a sign of guilt. Witches were bound and gagged and thrown into a pond of cold water. Those that floated were presumed guilty. The ones that sank, although considered innocent, were often dead by the time they were dragged out of the water.

"ALL I DID WAS COMPLAIN TO THE LANDLORD WE HADN'T GOT A BATHROOM !!

Dining out with Good King John

Perhaps the bloodiest dinner in history was given in 1356 at Rouen by King John the Good, who refused to eat until the heads of four of the guests he considered traitors were brought to him. The four were seized by guards and beheaded on the spot, after which the king dined heartily. One wonders what else he did to deserve the nickname "the good"

In England until 1547, poisoners were punished by being boiled to death. Mongolia, until not long ago, executed killers by sealing them alive in a wooden coffin and leaving them to die.

When the Danes occupied Ireland in the 9th Century, they imposed crippling taxes– and punished evaders by slashing their noses. This so-called "nose tax" inspired the idiom "to pay through the nose"

This Kid ain't kidding

Cowboy outlaw Billy the Kid's ambition was to kill a man for every year of his life – and he succeeded! The baby-faced gunman, born William H. Bonney, claimed his first victim in 1872, when he was only 12 years old. During the next nine years he took a bloody part in the Lincoln County cattle war in New Mexico. When he was finally shot dead by Sheriff Pat Garrett, he was aged 21 – and had murdered at least that many men.

Web of deceit

A spider painted on the ceiling of a room in the palace of Sans Souci, built by Frederick the Great near Potsdam in 1747, records an amazing true story. Frederick was about to drink his bedtime cup of hot chocolate when, overcome by a sneezing fit, he put it down and went to fetch a handkerchief. On his return, he

DOWN AND ACROSS

How to play

The answers in this puzzle are identical for down and across.

	1	2	3	4	5
1					
2					
3					
4					
5					

Clues

1. _ _ _ _ _ HEADS (Qld Sunshine Coast resort)
2. LIGHTNING RIDGE'S PRECIOUS GEMS
3. FERTILE SPOT
4. CUT FINELY
5. ADVANTAGE

Answers on Page 190

discovered that a spider had fallen into the cup. He called angrily to the cook to bring a fresh cup– but instead heard a cry of anguish followed by a pistol shot. The cook, who had been bribed to poison the drink, had shot himself – because he thought he had been found out!

"HAVE A HEART, MAN — THAT'S MY MOTHER-IN-LAW!"

Famous last words on the scaffold

Anne Boleyn, ill-fated bride of King Henry VIII, to a friend: "The executioner is, I believe, very expert– and my neck is very slender."

Danton, one of the leaders of the French Revolution, to the operator of the guillotine: "Be sure you show the mob my head. It will be a long time ere they see its like."

Marie Antoinette: "Farewell my children for ever. I am going to your father."

Her husband, **King Louis XVI**, to the crowd: "Frenchmen, I die guiltless of the crime crimes imputed to me. Pray God my blood fall not on France!"

Duke of Monmouth, to the executioner wielding an axe: "There are six guineas for you and do not hack me as you did my Lord Russell."

The **King of Naples** to the firing squad: "Soldiers, save my face – aim at my heart."

Bewitched?

Blokes certainly had some protection from female sorcery in the good old days. During the reign of Queen Elizabeth I (1533-1603) an edict proclaimed: "Any woman who through use of false hair, Spanish hair pads, make-up, false hips, steel busks, panniers, high-heeled shoes or other devices, leads a subject of Her Majesty in marriage, shall be punished with the penalties of witchcraft." In those days, that usually meant a horrible death.

Murder most (and least) foul

The Maldives boasts the lowest murder rate in the world. Not one of its citizens has been murdered since the small nation became independent in July 1965. Brazil, on the other hand, has around 370 murders a day.

Drawn-out death, indeed

The sentence pronounced on the five judges who condemned England's King Charles I to death: "You shall go from hence to the place from whence you came, and from that place shall be drawn upon a hurdle to the place of execution, and there shall hang by the neck till you are half dead, and shall be cut down alive, and your privy members cut off before your face an d thrown into the fire, your belly ripped up and your bowels burnt, your head to be severed from your body, your body shall be divided into four quarters, *and disposed as His Majesty shall think fit."*

And why did King Charles wear two shirts for his execution in the Banqueting Hall in Whitehall on 30 January 1649? Regal to the last, he feared that if he shivered with cold, his enemies would claim he had been afraid to face death.

WOW! THE IRON MAIDEN... THE WRACK... THUMB SCREWS ... FLOGGING ... CAN I HAVE A GO AT ALL OF THEM ?!

The Shearing of the COOK'S DOG

HENRY LAWSON'S CLASSIC OUTBACK TALE

THE DOG was a little conservative mongrel poodle, with long dirty white hair all over him – longest and most over his eyes, which glistened through it like black beads. Also he seemed to have a bad liver. He always looked as if he was suffering from a sense of injury, past or to come. It did come. He used to follow the shearers up to the shed after breakfast every morning, but he couldn't have done this for love – there was none lost between him and the men. He wasn't an affectionate dog; it wasn't his style. He would sit close against the shed wall for an hour or two, and hump himself, and sulk, and look sick, and snarl whenever the "Sheep-Ho" dog passed, or a man took notice of him. Then he'd go home. What he wanted at the shed at all was only known to himself; no one asked him to come. Perhaps he came to collect evidence against us. The cook called him "my darg," and the men called the cook "Curry-and-Rice," with "old" before it mostly.

Curry-and-Rice was a little, dumpy, fat man, with a round, smooth, good-humoured face, a bald head, feet wide apart, and a big blue cotton apron. He had been a ship's cook. He didn't look so much out of place in the hut as the hut did round him. To a man with a vivid imagination, if he regarded the cook dreamily for a while, the floor might seem to roll gently like the deck of a ship, and mast, rigging, and cuddy rise mistily in the background. Curry might have dreamed of the cook's galley at times, but he never mentioned it. He ought to have been at sea, or comfortably dead and stowed away under ground, instead of cooking for a mob of unredeemed rouseabouts in an uncivilized shed in the scrub, six hundred miles from the ocean.

They chyacked the cook occasionally, and grumbled – or pretended to grumble – about their tucker, and then he'd make a roughly pathetic speech, with many references to his age, and the hardness of his work, and the smallness of his wages, and the inconsiderateness of the men. Then the joker of the shed would sympathize with the cook with his tongue and one side of his face – and joke with the other.

One day in the shed, during smoke-ho the devil whispered to a shearer named Geordie that it would be a lark to shear the cook's dog – the Evil One having previously arranged that the dog should be there, sitting close to Geordie's pen, and that the shearer should have a fine lamb comb on his machine. The idea was communicated through Geordie to his mates, and met with the entire and general approval; and for five or ten minutes the air was kept alive by shouting and laughter of the men, and the protestations of the dog. When the shearer touched skin, he yelled "Tar!" and when he finished he shouted "Wool away!" at the top of his voice, and his mates echoed him with a will. A picker-up gathered the fleece with a great show of labour and care, and tabled it, to the well-ventilated disgust of old Scotty, the wool-roller. When they let the dog go he struck for home – a clean-shaven poodle, except for a ferocious moustache and a tuft at the end of his tail.

The cook's assistant said that he'd have given a five-pound note for a portrait of Curry-and-Rice when that poodle came back from the shed. The cook was naturally very indignant; he was surprised at first – then he got mad. He had the whole afternoon to get worked up in, and at tea-time he went for the men properly.

"Wotter yer growl'in' about?" asked one. "Wot's the matter with yer, anyway?"

"I don't know nothing about yer dog!" protested a rouseabout; "wotyer gettin' on to me for?"

"Wotter they bin doin' to the cook now?" inquired a ringleader innocently, as he sprawled into his place at the table. "Can't yer let Curry alone? Wot dyer want to be chyackin' him for? Give it a rest."

"Well, look here, chaps," observed Geordie, in a determined tone, "I call it a shame, that's what I call it. Why couldn't you leave an old man's dog alone? It was a mean, dirty trick to do, and I suppose you thought it funny. You ought to be ashamed of yourselves, the whole lot of you, for a drafted mob of crawlers. If I'd been there it wouldn't have been done; and I wouldn't blame Curry if he was to poison the whole convicted push."

General lowering of faces and pulling of hats down over eyes, and great working of knives and forks; also sounds like men trying not to laugh.

"Why couldn't you play a trick on another man's darg?" said Curry. "It's no use tellin' me. I can see it all as plain as if I was on the board – all of you runnin' and shoutin' an' cheerin' an' laughin', and all over shearin' and ill-usin' a poor little darg! Why couldn't you play a trick on another man's darg? ... It doesn't matter much – I'm nearly done cookin' here now ... Only that I've got a family to think of I wouldn't 'a' stayed so long. I've got to be up at five every mornin', an' don't get to bed till ten at night, cookin' an' bakin' an' cleanin' for you an' waitin' on you. First one lot in from the wool-wash, an' then one lot in from the shed, an' another lot in, an' at all hours an' times, an' all wantin' their meals kept hot, an' then they ain't satisfied. And now you must go an' play a dirty trick on my darg! Why couldn't you have a lark with some other man's darg!"

Geordie bowed his head and ate as though he had a cud, like a cow, and would chew at leisure. He seemed ashamed, as indeed we all were – secretly. Poor old Curry's oftrepeated appeal, "Why couldn't you play a trick with another man's dog?" seemed to have something pathetic about it. The men didn't notice that it lacked philanthropy and logic, and probably the cook didn't notice it either, else he wouldn't have harped on it. Geordie lowered his face, and just then, as luck would have it, he caught sight of the dog. He exploded.

The cook usually forgot all about it in an hour, and then, if you asked him what the chaps had been doing, he'd say, "Oh, nothing! nothing! Only their larks!" But this time he didn't; he was narked for three days, and the chaps marve'lled much and were sorry, and treated him with great respect and consideration. They hadn't thought he'd take it so hard – the dog-shearing business – else they wouldn't have done it. They were a little puzzled, too, and getting a trifle angry, and would shortly be prepared to take the place of the injured party, and make things unpleasant for the cook. However, he brightened up towards the end of the week, and then it all came out.

"I wouldn't 'a' minded so much," he said, standing by the table with a dipper in one hand, a bucket in the other, and a smile on his face. "I wouldn't 'a' minded so much only they'll think me a flash man in Bourke with that theer darg trimmed up like that!" #

STOP PRESS?

A "QUEEN" INSPECTS HER FAIRIES

CRUMBLING PILES

Owners held to blame

FLIES TO HAVE TWINS IN IRELAND

WOMEN LAY OBSERVERS AT COUNCIL

VATICAN PROPOSAL BY CARDINAL

FROM OUR OWN CORRESPONDENT

ROME, Oct. 22

His Gas Comes From A Hole

Natural Supply In Area

Earlier today Mr. Macmillan and Mr. Heath had an audience with Pope John.—Reuter.

Pope unwell

Amazing facts about SEX!

EVER MET a monorchid male? You will if you go to Botswana, where several tribes of bushmen sport only one testicle each. By the way, if you're a Caucasian male, chances are that you are diorchid.

Mating games

Cobras take between two minutes and 24 hours to mate, while snails can keep at it for up to 12 hours. Impala often copulate on the run.

When a male California sea otter grasps the nose of a female otter between his teeth, it's a signal that he wants to mate– and he keeps holding her down with his teeth until it's all over.

Birds and the bees ... and lots more

Sex changes come easily to oysters – they alternate between being male and female regularly during their lifetime. But the most common hermaphrodite is the garden worm – it boasts both male and female organs on its body.

Gorillas not only have much shorter noses than humans, but the average length of a gorilla penis when erect is a mere 5 cm. But which animal has the most complicated erect penis? Not the human or the gorilla – it's the tiny rabbit flea. As you would expect, the elephant boasts the world's largest penis – which on average weighs 27kg.

The French love snails, but have you ever wondered why snails don't go in for French kissing? Simple: a snail's teeth run lengthwise along it's tongue, which makes tongue kissing a sore point, to say the least.

My oath!

The English word testimony has a very unusual origin. When ancient Romans swore an oath to tell the truth, they solemnly placed their right hand on their testicles. Only after that were they allowed to give evidence.

Pressure of work

English greyhound Low Pressure proved that you can't judge a dog by its name. Low Pressure holds the world record for canine procreation: between December 1961 and his death in November 1969, he sired at least 3014 pups. In between, he also won a few races.

A kiss is just a kiss ...

The world's first open-mouthed kiss on screen saw real-life lovers Greta Garbo and John Gilbert titillate moviegoers in "Flesh and the Devil", which premiered on 9 January 1927 But kissing on screen is banned in Turkey because authorities fear it will lead to promiscuity.

The Medieval Catholic Church had a much bigger problem when

it tried desperately to stamp out any but the "missionary" position of sexual intercourse. Using the "canine" approach, which was particularly favoured by the masses, called for seven years of penance!

Don't be naughty

To prevent masturbation early last century, fathers fitted small cages around their son's genitals, like a male chastity belt. J. L. Milton's Victorian best-seller, *Spermatorrhea*, details genital cages (illustrated below) lined with spikes, which were worn at night, and

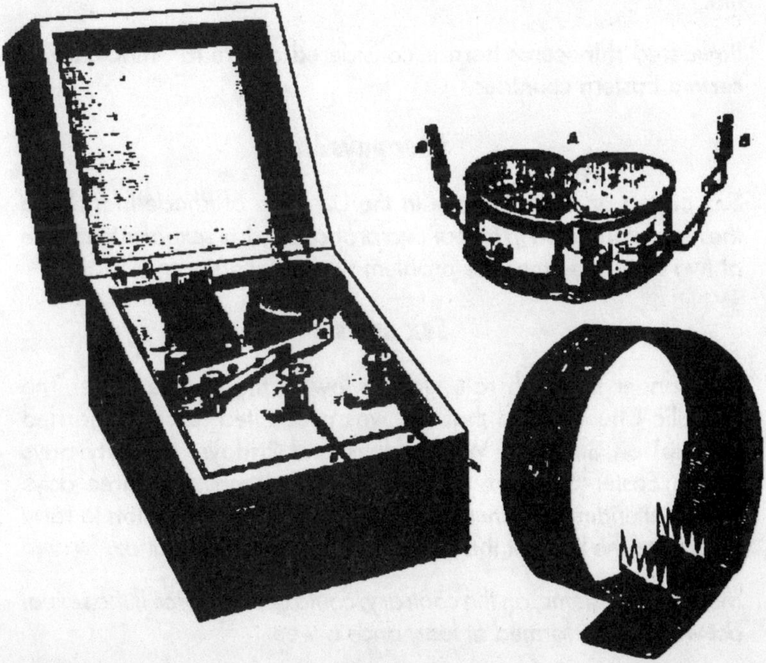

a special electric device immediately triggered a bell which rang in the parents' room when the son had an erection!

Long live sex!

According to the communist Bible, the "China Daily", sex is good for old people. It said recent studies by Chinese experts had shown that sex was a "special medicine" which helped slow down the aging process and prevent some medical problems. Sex also helped many old people "cope with the problems of everyday life" The newspaper reported that a survey of 1000 readers between sixty and seventy showed that sixty per cent were still having a sex life.

Powdered rhinoceros horn is considered a cure for impotency in certain Eastern countries.

User pays?

Sex pays – or it would have in the US State of Rhode Island had the legislators voted in favour of a proposal to tax sexual intercourse at two dollars a time. The problem was enforcing payments.

Sex and sin

No wonder the birth rate was so low in the Middle Ages! The Catholic Church ruled that sex was prohibited (even to married couples) on Sundays, Wednesdays and Fridays, for forty days before Easter and forty days before Christmas, for three days before attending communion, from the time of conception to forty days after the birth of the baby, and during any penance.

Medieval Moslems, on the contrary, could get a divorce if the sexual act was not performed at least once a week.

Codswallop?

Not surprisingly, randy King Henry VIII's armour has the largest codpiece on display in the Tower of London. Below are some examples of this amazing medieval fashion which saw men, rather than women, flaunt their physical attributes.

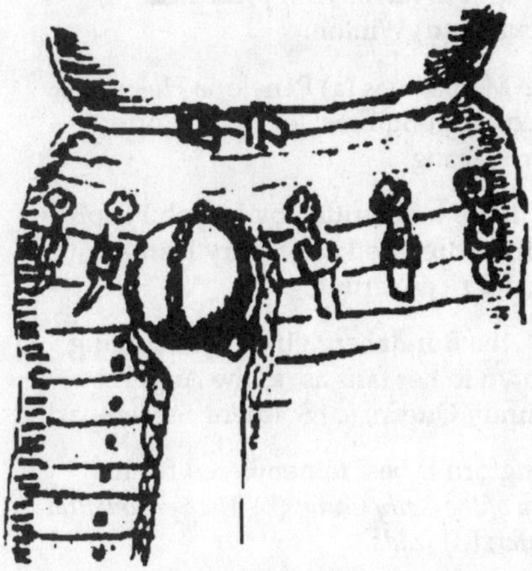

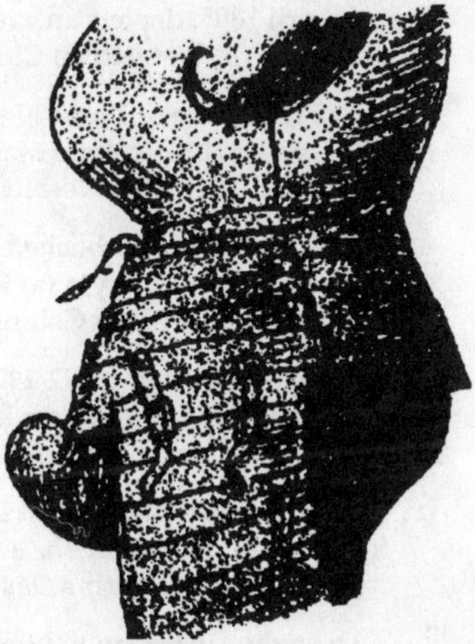

WOW!

Don Juan's name is synonymous with that of a great lover, but how many mistresses did the legendary 14th Century Spanish nobleman have? According to Mozart, in his opera Don Giovanni, *the insatiable libertine regularly made love to 700 women in Italy, 800 in Germany, 91 in Turkey and France, and 1003 in Spain.*

And silent movie actress Clara Bow once proved her sexual prowess by taking on an entire university football team.

Showbiz & Art Quiz

1 Aussie-born Errol Flynn won his first major role in Charles Chauvel's 1933 movie (a) *Mutiny on the Bounty*; (b) *In the wake of the Bounty;* (c) *Captain Blood;* (d) *My Wicked, Wicked Ways.*

2 Banjo Paterson's *Waltzing Matilda,* first sung in public at a pub on 6 April 1895, depicts an event said to have taken place near (a) Bourke; (b) Walgett; (c) Cloncurry; (d) Winton.

3 The real name of Dame Nellie Melba, was (a) Penelope Helen O'Dwyer; (b) Penelope Marlborough-Squires; (c) Helen Porter Mitchell; (d) Nellie Nesbitt Armstrong.

4 *Such is Life,* first published in 1903, was written by Joseph Furphy under the pseudonym (a) Rolf Boldrewood; (b) Henry Handel Richardson; (c) Tom Collins; (d) Price Warung.

5 Gladys Moncrieff (1892-1976), the Bundaberg girl whose singing enchanted Australia, was known to her fans as (a) the Angel's Voice; (b) Our Glad; (c) the Bundy Queen; (d) Soldiers' Sweetheart.

6 Aussie director Raymond Longford is best remembered for his 1919 silent movie (a) *The Story of the Kelly Gang;* (b) *The Sentimental Bloke;* (c) *The Squatter's Daughter;* (d) *Jedda.*

7 The only Australian to be awarded the Nobel Prize for Literature, in 1973, was former jackeroo (a) Xavier Herbert; (b) Norman Lindsay; (c) Patrick White; (d) Frank Hardy.

8 Australia's internationally celebrated opera star Joan Sutherland is married to the pianist and conductor Richard (a) Bradford; (b) Bentley; (c) Sutherland; (d) Bonynge.

9 The controversial painting by American Jackson Pollock (1912-56), which was bought in September 1973 by the Australian National Gallery for the record sum of $1.3 million, is titled (a) Bluebirds; (b) Blue Poles; (c) Blue Skies; (d) Blue Fish.

10 *While the Billy Boils,* published in 1896, is a collection of writings by by (a) Henry Lawson; (b) A.B. "Banjo" Paterson; (c) Joseph Furphy; (d) Henry Handel Richardson.

11 Australia's most famous literary hoax, published in *Angry Penguins* in 1944, allegedly featured the work of the poet (a) Ern Malley; (b) Lindsay Adams; (c) Henry Lawson; (d) Xavier Herbert.

12 The author of *We of the Never Never* was (a) Jeannie (Mrs Aneas) Gunn; (b) Louisa Alcott; (c) Sheila (Mrs Siegfried) Waterford; (d) Henry Handel Richardson.

13 The Felton Bequest, Australia's finest art collection, is housed in the (a) Library of New South Wales; (b) National Gallery of Victoria; (c) Adelaide University; (d) Art Gallery of Queensland.

14 Jedda, the first Australian colour feature film, was made by (a) Pat Hanna; (b) Norman Dawn; (c) Frank Hurley; (d) Charles Chauvel.

15 The Australian Country Music Awards has been held each January since 1973 in (a) Lismore (NSW); (b) Maryborough (Vic); (c) Tamworth (NSW); (d) Orbost (Vic).

16 The Steele Rudd characters Dad and Dave made their stage debut in May 1912 in the play (a) *Currency Lads;* (b) *Sentimental Blokes;* (c) *On Our Selection;* (d) *Farming Frolics.*

17 William Dobell retained the Archibald Prize in 1943 despite a court challenge alleging that he had created a caricature, not a portrait, of fellow artist (a) Joshua Smith; (b) Arthur Murch; (c) Henry Hanke; (d) Normand Baker.

18 The first Australian single to appear on the US pop charts, in September 1962, was Frank Ifield's (a) *Yes Sir, That's My Baby*; (b) *Friday On My Mind*; (c) *I'll Remember You*; (d) *I'll Step Down*.

19 Director Peter Weir is well known for *Gallipoli* (1981) and his 1975 film (a) *Sunday Too Far Away;* (b) *Picnic at Hanging Rock;* (c) *Mad Max;* (d) *The Chant of Jimmy Blacksmith.*

20 The Little Black Princess, written by Mrs Aneas Gunn and published in 1905, is set on a cattle station in (a) western NSW; (b) the Northern Territory; (c) Queensland; (d) Western Australia..

Answers on Page 190

Sexy fun!

"I KNOW WE'RE DESPERADOS, ELI – BUT WE SURE AIN'T THAT DESPERATE!"

"A CLEAR CASE OF MISREPRESENTATION!"

"... SOMEWHERE YOU CAN TAKE ALL YOUR CLOTHES OFF AND GET BACK TO NATURE – HOW ABOUT MY PLACE?"

My word! What's in a NAME?

EVER seen a furphy? Of course not – any fair dinkum Aussie knows a furphy is a word used to describe an idle rumour, so how could you possibly see it? Well, you would if you come across a classic metal-bodied water cart made by the firm of John Furphy and Sons at their foundry in Shepparton, Victoria, early this century.

During the First World War, Furphy water carts (originally designed for use on farms) were used to supply water in Australian military camps, mainly for sanitation purposes.

They became popular meeting places for soldiers, and the camp rumours that originated around them soon came to be called furphies.

Each Furphy water cart proudly carried the slogan of the company at the bottom of the tank near the tap:

Good, better, best,
never let it rest,
till your good is better,
and your better – best.

Amazingly, around the turn of the century, author Joseph Furphy (a member of the John Furphy family) had published his famous work, *Such Is Life*, under the pen-name Tom Collins – which at that timewas *a synonym for a baseless rumour!*

What's in a name?

Who was Tweedledum and Tweedledee? Fictional characters, actually, used in a verse by the satirist John Byron in the 18th Century as nicknames for two quarreling groups of musicians who really held much the same opinions. Instead of being in opposite camps, they were as alike as Tweedledum and Tweedledee.

Cockney rhyming slang has given English many of its best known – and most mystifying – idioms. A prime example is "Not on your Nellie" To figure out its meaning, you need to know that Cockney slang for life is "puff": in rhyming slang "Not on your puff" becomes "Not on your Nellie Duff" But, to baffle completely those born beyond the sound of the Bow Bells, the rhyming word is usually discarded, so that the expression ends up as "Not on your Nellie!" Similarly, "use your loaf" comes from loaf of bread rhyming with head.

A local law in Sienna, Italy, bans anyone named Mary from being a prostitute.

Calling someone a "son of a gun" is not as jocular a greeting as you may think – strictly speaking, you're casting doubt on his parentage. The phrase originally was one of contempt for a person born on board a Royal Navy ship in the days when women were allowed to accompany their sailor sweethearts. When giving birth, the women were placed behind a canvas screen, usually near one of the midships guns; if the name of the father was doubtful, the baby was entered in the ship's log as "Son (or daughter) of a gun"

The ever-popular sandwich got its name from John Montagu, 4th Earl of Sandwich, a compulsive gambler who was First Lord of the Admiralty during the American Revolution. In 1762, while engrossed at a gambling table for more than 24 hours, he ordered

'IF HE'S A MAN OF SUCH GREAT VISION,
WHY IS HE WEARING SPECTACLES ?'

thin pieces of ham between two slices of bread so he could eat without interrupting the play. The dish soon became fashionable as the sandwich.

Of ships and sailing folk

Why does someone "spin a yarn" when telling a tall tale? The saying originated in the great days of sail, when sailors would amuse each other while making ropes from spun yarn by telling stories about their adventures.

The first "posh" people were those wealthy enough to afford cabins on the shady side of ships sailing from England to countries such as Australia and India. Their tickets were endorsed POSH, an acronym for "Port Out, Starboard Home"

You could have fooled me

Do you realise that only politicians are not idiots? If you think that's an idiotic statement, you're in for a surprise. Originally in Greece the word idiot meant any person not holding a public office. Of course, in those days of pure democracy being a politician was an honour.

SHADY CHARACTERS

How to play: Unscramble these five Australian towns or cities . When you have solved the puzzle, the shaded letters will spell out a sixth.

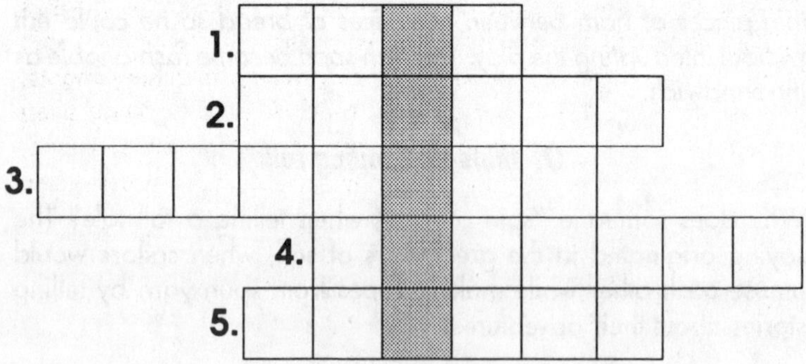

Clues

1. **AMOR (Qld)**
2. **BOOMER (WA)**
3. **TARABALL (Vic)**
4. **KERRMAN (SA)**
5. **HAZEEN (Tas)**

Answers on Page 190

Walking tall in the BIG COUNTRY

LIVING on the world's biggest island certainly is a big deal – and in case anyone should miss the point, our Big Country has been covered with decorations of truly epic proportions. They tell of our agricultural achievements, our heroes and villains, our animals (and a few that never even graced our fair land), our legends, fish, drinking habits, sports, footwear – even that machine vital to every suburban garden, the lawn mower.

To some they represent the ultimate in kitsch, but these garish gargantuans are undeniably eye-catching tributes to some of our biggest achievements.

Queensland leads the field in the farming stakes, and in other areas as well: the big strawberry near Brisbane, the big cow at Yandina, and two big pineapples, one at Gympie and the other near Nambour.

Although the fibreglass Gympie giant is by far the biggest – 16 metres high and 7.62 metres in diameter – it is overshadowed in popularity by the equally fruity walk-in model near the Sunshine Coast. Each year well over a million people, most of them sipping pineapple juice, walk through its two floors of audio-visual displays which tell the story of the State's tropical fruits. The 5.5 metre tall pineapple is set in the Sunshine Plantation, a working pineapple farm where visitors can tour the crop by miniature train.

A tale of a different kind is told in the display area inside the belly of Yandina's big cow, an 8 metre high and nearly 11 metre long monstrous moo with teats like stalactites. And, almost made to measure for the cow, there is an outsize model of a bullfrog bell (worn by cattle to make their presence known in the bush) at a picnic reserve at Condamine, also in Queensland.

Berri, in South Australia, sports an enormous navel orange, weighing 125 tonnes and claimed to be the world's biggest; New South Wales is represented by Coffs Harbour's big banana and Batlow's big apple.

Fishy claims to greatness also abound. Approaching Cairns, in northern Queensland, drivers are confronted by a shimmering black marlin, its 20 towering metres paying tribute to the town's reputation as the game-fishing capital of the world. Hard on its heels (in size, not proximity) is Larry the leviathan lobster. He's part of a complex at Kingston, South Australia, which includes a seafood restaurant, aquarium and auditorium where visitors can watch films showing a day in the life of a fisherman.

The Premier State, too, is well represented, with Wagga Wagga and Tocumwal each boasting a giant cod, and Adaminaby's 12 metre trout easily trouncing the one that graces the town of Horsham, Victoria.

But what is food without drink? To keep the balance, the world's biggest bottle has been erected at Freshwater Creek, near Geelong in Victoria. It was made from 17,000 soft-drink bottles and inside it there is a staircase that enables children to reach the top of a slide and have an exciting ride down.

If your thirst is for something stronger, never fear. Griffith, in New South Wales, has a giant wine bottle, 17 metres long and 4 metres in diameter, and a giant wine barrel; while an outsize stubby cooler at Smithville, near Cairns, commemorates the great

The Big Lobster, Kingston, S.A.

Australian beer-drinking tradition. Inside the cooler, naturally, is a stubby bottle of suitable dimensions.

Big animals range from life-size dinosaurs at Coonabarabran (New South Wales) and Nambour (Queensland), to a huge Northern Territory buffalo on the Stuart Highway near Darwin, a cassowary and her chicks at Mission Beach South (Queensland), a big hen (Blackwood, Victoria), a big ram (Campbell Town, Tasmania) and a big horse (Vineyard, New South Wales). The town of Penguin, Tasmania, is dominated by – you guessed it – a giant penguin.

Mythical monsters, too, have their place in our unusual gallery of greatness. At Murray Bridge, South Australia, a bunyip roars when fed a coin, and so does its brother (sister?) at Albury.

Of course, Australia would not be the same without a monument to Ned Kelly, and a towering statue of the iron-clad bushranger has been erected near the site of his famous last stand at Glenrowan, Victoria. To balance the scales of greatness, Cairns has an equally tall statue of a different kind of hero: Captain James Cook.

The thousands of gold miners, whose back-breaking labours changed the face of Australia, are remembered by the 4.5 metre high gold panner outside Bathurst, New South Wales.

Sport, too, is represented in a big way, with Wagga Wagga's big football, big golf balls in Melbourne and Tweed Heads, and several giant bowling pins scattered throughout the country.

Then there is the big rocking horse (Gumeracha, South Australia), the big boot (Brisbane), the big walking stick and hand (Collingwood, Victoria), the big mower (Beerwah, Queensland), the big shell (Tewantin, Queensland), the world's biggest talking Humpty Dumpty (Mildura, Victoria) ...

All over Australia the products of big thinking continue to flourish. Perhaps they will never be regarded as architectural masterpieces, but they are certainly hard to miss!

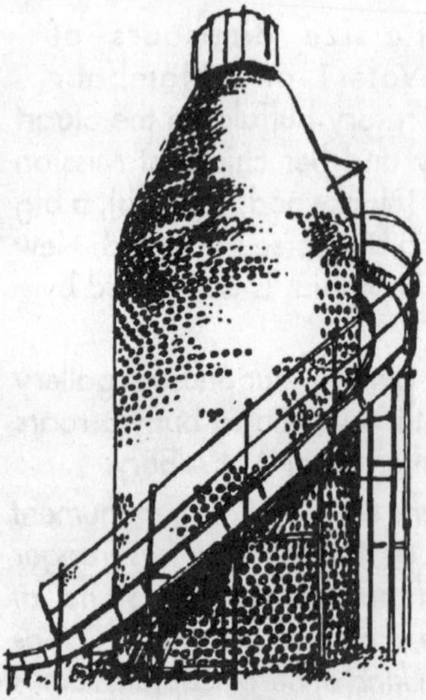

The Big Bottle

The Big Pineapple

Eat, drink and be merry

THE FULL saying, of course, is *Eat, drink and be merry, for tomorrow we die*. Or is it? Actually, this popular idiom is a combination of two Biblical sayings: '...a man hath no better thing under the sun, than to eat, and to drink, and to be merry' (*Ecclesiastes 8:15*), and 'let us eat and drink; for tomorrow we shall die' (*Isaiah 22:13*).

While on a Biblical note, when Queen Elizabeth I, way back in 1601, made eating with a fork fashionable, the clergy accused her of insulting God by not touching his bounty with her fingers. And as late as 1842, a book on etiquette advised: "Ladies may wipe their lips on the tablecloth, but not blow their noses with it."

Food for thought

In 1896, Russia's Czar Nicholas II dined on the meat of an extinct woolly mammoth, which had been deep frozen in Siberia for thousands of years. It reportedly tasted something between bear and whale meat.

The favourite entree at an Eskimo dinner is whale skin complete with a greasy layer of blubber.

In Tanzania, a popular dessert is a pie made by mixing squashed white ants with dried and powdered banana.

The proof of the spirit...

Most people who indulge in a tipple know that spirits are a certain percentage proof, which indicates the relative quantities of water and alcohol in the mixture. Scientifically, proof spirit has a specific gravity of 12 over 13 at 51 degrees Fahrenheit. The original proof test employed a more practical kind of science: spirit poured over gunpowder and lit would eventually fire the powder if it was proof; if under-proof, the water remaining after the alcohol had burned off would prevent the powder from igniting.

Australia's first brewery was established by John Boston, who used maize and the leaves and stalks of the Cape gooseberry to brew beer in 1796 in Sydney. The first government brewery was opened in Parramatta in 1804.

This dog won't bite

Why do people refer to the morning-after drink that cures a hangover as "a hair of the dog that bit you"? In the days when superstition and medical science were one, it was believed that the bite from a mad dog could be cured by putting some of its hairs on the wound.

If you were a Roman Romeo, you would have needed a mad dog's hairs regularly, because having a sweetheart with a long name could easily turn you into a drunk. When toasting her, tradition demanded that you drink a cup of wine for each letter in her name.

Why do we say ...

Eat humble pie: Fancy feasting on the heart, liver and entrails

'..AND YOU SOLEMNLY SWEAR THIS PIE IS MEAT, WHOLE MEAT AND NOTHING BUT MEAT!!'

of a deer? Known collectively as the umbles, they were invariably baked into a pie after a hunt and dished up for the lower orders during the Middle Ages – while the Lord and his household dined on the choice cuts of venison. This eventually became known as humble pie.

Baker's dozen: *In years gone by the law prescribed severe penalties for anyone selling bread below a specified weight. Scales were not always accurate, so to protect themselves, bakers counted 13 to the dozen. The extra loaf supplied with each dozen was known as the "vantage loaf".*

Eve tempted Adam with an apple: According to the Bible, she did not. Genesis never mentions an apple, but merely "the fruit of the tree which is in the midst of the garden" A tomato, too, was mistaken by Spaniards for a kind of apple when they discovered it in South America. Not only did it taste good, but appeared to boost the homesick adventurers' sagging morale to such an extent they enthusiastically called it the love apple. (Scientists, alas, insist the tomato has no aphrodisiac qualities – so obviously the South American ladies were the real morale boosters.)

Barefoot Bob in Melbourne

by Tom Collins

HALF-WAY TO the station, I met a horseman, followed by a loose pack-horse; a lean, wiry-looking man, whose sun-darkened face and hands contrasted amusingly with his white boots and stylish city garments. I had to look over him carefully, as he approached, before fully recognizing another friend of former days, though of much later date than Fred.

"Bob himself!" I exclaimed, as we met.

"Go to (sheol)!" responded Barefooted Bob delightedly. "Where you off to?"

"Railway station, to meet a friend. But I'm in no hurry. Where are you off to?"

A look of tranquillity settled on Bob's face. "Jist as fur back as I can git," he replied quietly and decisively.

"But you'll stay in Echuca tonight?"

"Didn't intend. But I'd like to have a pitch with you – sposen I wouldn't be in your road." So saying, he dismounted, and accompanied me back to Mrs. Ferguson's, leading his horse.

Bob, with the bushman's habitual taciturnity, had the bushman's artless candour. When the spell of silence was broken, he would tell you, not only anything he thought might interest you, but everything that interested himself. He had just passed a fortnight of utter desolation in Melbourne, and was now returning with all speed to the more cheerful and homelike regions of the Never-Never. Reaching Echuca by the midday train, he had straightway gone to the paddock for his horses, with a view to Deniliquin Common as his next camp.

"Wouldn't live in that hell-upon-earth, not if you give me a pension," he remarked fervidly. "This was my fust sight of the curse o' God's wilderness, an' I swear it'll be the last. I'm on'y sorry for the people that's tied up to it. Even the ships was a have. Why, they're no size. I always thought a ship was as long as from here to that pointed church, an' as wide as from here to where that dray's standin' " (The distance first indicated was about a quarter of a mile; the last, about a hundred yards.) "Decenter finished than I thought, though. I expected to see the mark o' the adze all over them; but they're touched off like buggies, an' most o' them solid iron. But once seein' them's enough, an' once seein' Melb'n's once too often. An' ain't the sea a swindle! Hear lots o' skitin' about sea-bathin' - well, I tried it one night last week, when there was nobody about; an' I'm blest if my rags ain't stickin' to my hide ever since. I'd rather stop dirty than fall back on that specie of cleanness. Fact is, the sea ain't fit to bogey in, it's too salt to drink, an' it ain't salt enough to keep properly. It's goin' rotten fast. An' I got my own opinion about the sea-breeze, from this out. My word!"

"So you didn't appreciate Melbourne," I observed, as we resumed our way to the station.

"Well, it ain't altogether like what I expect heaven to be, sposen I'm lucky enough to git there. Certainly, the Waxworks is splendid; I used to have a look through it every time I passed; but, outside o' that, you can see everything worth seein' in a couple of hours."

"Art galleries?" I suggested. "Turn out better work myself, if I had a fortnit's practice," replied Bob confidently. "Who wants to see a picture of a 'Sunrise', or a 'Winter Evening', when you can git the genuine article for nothing? As for the statutes – I wonder the bobbies allow them."

"Of course, you went to the theatre?"

"Rather. But one trip left me full up."

"What was the play?"

"Hamlet, I think – yes, Hamlet. The front part might a' been worth seein': but I was on'y in time to git the tailend. The blokes on the stage acts right enough, but they can't recite worth sixpence. One o' them happened to spout my own favourite recitation; an' it would give you the influenza to watch his gyvers. Course, you know the words as well as I do:–

"AlasporeYorickIknewhimwellHoratio'–

"An' so on. Well, this cove, with his black tights an' black poncho, he turns the skull over in the hands for a bit, then he looks across the country at nothing, like a feller in a dream; an' by-an'-by he says,

"'Alas!'

"Then he looks down at the skull agen; an' after a while he says,

"'P-o-r-e Yorick!'

"Studies a bit longer, then turns partly round to the other galoot, an' remarks in a mournful tone o' voice,

"'I knew him well, Horatio.' Another bit of a think; then he gits a move on agen – 'A fine fellow of infinite jest, of most excellent fancy; has borne me on his back a thousand times' an' cetera.

"An' while this was goin' on, about an acre of people was watchin' an' lis'nin', an' tryin' to git the worth o' their money. I was fair disgusted."

"You should have followed it up every night, Bob, till you got properly in touch," I suggested.

"I bettered that," replied the Goth drily. "Opera – no less. Yes; I've seen a opera, an' I'm quite satisfied. My word! I forgit the name o' the performance – foreign gibberage, anyhow. Fust, a woman comes on the stage, dressed up to the nines, an' sings something, with music goin' all the time; then comes a bloke, dolled up like's if he'd come out of a ban'-box, an' he sings some parley voo to the woman; an' she sings something back to him. But while these two was actin' the goat, an' the music keepin' time with them, in comes another cove wearin' the same rig-out; an' he sings something to the fust feller; an' the fust feller sings something back to him. Then each o' them draws a sword about as wide as a saddle-strap, an' they fought to a brisk, lively sort o' music. Next, the woman runs in between them, an' sings something to the second chap; an' he sings back to her; an' the fust bloke chips in with his Last-Rose-of-Summer – That settled me.

"'Here!' says I to the swell-cove sittin' aside me – 'let me git out! This is deadly!' An' out I got. Yes. I can stand a lot o' common foolishness; but I'd want ten bob an hour for seein' operas."

**Tom Collins was the pseudonym of Joseph Furphy (1843-1912).*

WORD BUILDING

Begin with the first word in column "A", then select a word from column "B" and then one from column "C", in that order, so that three small words form one large word. For example: COOL-ANG-ATTA would form Coolangatta. All answers are towns or cities of Australia.

	A	B	C
1.	COOL	LON	NONG
2.	GUN	LING	ATTA
3.	WOL	HAMP	TON
4.	COL	CES	INE
5.	DAN	ANG	TON
6.	ROCK	DA	WOOD
7.	LAUN	ER	GONG
8.	KATH	DE	GAI

1. COOLANGATTA
2. ____________
3. ____________
4. ____________
5. ____________
6. ____________
7. ____________
8. ____________

Answers on Page 190

Let's face it, we're a weird lot

BEAUTY, they say, is in the eye of the beholder. And, in mankind's quest for what some consider beauty, we have done truly amazing things to improve what nature dished out – as the oddball and inventive characters we look at below make only too clear.

A tooth for a tooth?

English entrepreneur John Hunter, for instance, made a small fortune in the 18th Century transplanting teeth from the poor to the rich, who were the only ones who could afford sugar and thus suffered dental decay. Hunter charged five pounds five shillings (then several months' wages) for transplanting a live tooth (freshly ripped from a peasant's mouth) and half that for a corpse's tooth.

Poor George Washington went through life wearing badly fitting false teeth – and the results are still to be seen in his portrait that appears on American banknotes. The strange puffed appearance around the Washington's chin was caused not by mumps, but by rolls of cotton stuffed into his mouth when he sat for the portrait in an attempt to soften the protruding dentures. Washington wore dentures made from walrus ivory mounted in pure gold.

Leonardo da Vinci did not only paint the Mona Lisa, he also fitted the real-life model with a pair of dentures after she lost three of her own teeth midway through sittings. The shining replacement teeth were taken from corpses (a common practice in those days) and set in a copper frame designed by da Vinci.

And Queen Elizabeth I (also known incorrectly as the Virgin Queen) refused to smile in public towards the end of her life because her teeth were completely black. Her addiction to sugar and sweets caused the tooth decay.

'TO BE HONEST, SIR — I DID HAVE DIFFICULTY READING THE WRITING ON YOUR PRESCRIPTION ...'

Fuzzy faces

The pianist and composer Chopin, legend has it, shaved only one side of his face. Why? Because, he said, the audience could not

STEP LADDER

The last letter of each answer is the first letter of the next.

CLUES

1. **1930 Melb. Cup winner.**
2. **Aust. marsupial.**
3. **Melb. festival.**
4. **Former NSW premier.**
5. **Aust. Artist Sidney _____.**
6. **Australian Aboriginal artist.**
7. **_____ Springs.**
8. **Religious holiday.**
9. **Aust parrot.**

Answers on Page 191

see the other while he played.

Do you suffer from pogonophobia? If you fear beards, you qualify for the title. Russia's first Czar, Peter the Great, obviously suffered from the phobia, because he tried to stamp out hairy faces among his subjects by heavily taxing all beards. When that did not work, he ordered that anyone found with a beard be shaved with a blunt razor or have every bristle pulled out with tweezers.

When Shakespeare in *A Midsummer Night's Dream* mentions a character's "straw colour beard", he is referring to a popular fashion in Elizabethan England which involved men dying their beards and, more frequently, their moustaches in colours ranging from yellow to red, orange and purple.

... and nose jobs

Ever heard of the men with the golden noses? History records at least two, both of whom had their own beaks slashed off in duels. Seventeenth century Danish astronomer Tycho Brahe took off his solid gold nose when he went to bed at night, gluing it back into position each morning. And when Roman Emperor Justinian II cleaned his golden nose, it was a sign he would execute someone.

Royal recipes

Humans shed skin just like snakes – but a lot more often. Almost invisible bits of dead skin are constantly being rubbed off, with scientific tests showing we lose a complete outer layer every four weeks. To keep her skin looking fresh, 4th Century French Queen Isabeau used a complexion cream made of crocodile glands, boar's brains and wolf's blood. Madame Tallien, a courtesan of King Louis IV, kept her skin sexy by bathing in crushed strawberries.

'...AS A PASSING OUT CEREMONY, I THINK IT'S A BIT HIT AND MISS'

How weird can you get?

For a few years last century it was the height of fashion for women to wear rings, often decorated with jewels. But not on their fingers – they specially pierced their nipples for this purpose.

King Charles II's favourite wigs were made from the pubic hair of his mistresses.

Anne Boleyn, wife of King Henry VIII, had three breasts (and six fingers). The King was not impressed – he had her head removed.

The buttock is the largest muscle in the human body. Surveys around the world have also consistently revealed that women consider the sexiest part of a man is his buttocks – particularly if they are small.

Brazilian Shakespeare fan Juan Potomachi bequeathed 20,000 pesos and his head to the Teatro Dramatico in Buenos Aires, on condition that his skull be used for that of Yorick in every production of Hamlet. The theatre company agreed to the deal.

DROP DOWN

HOW TO PLAY

The letters in each vertical column go into the squares directly below them, but not necessarily in the order they appear. A black square indicates the end of a word. When you have placed all the letters in their correct squares, you will be able to read a wise old proverb.

E	E	H	O	O	N	I	A	C	Y	R	L	S	S
T	N	Y	C	U	M	O	N	N	I	E	A	E	E
K	T	E	P		N	U	M	B	E	L	L		M
			E			P	T		R				
K	E	E	P	■				■				■	
		■								■			
	■				■								
■				■							■	■	■

Answers on Page 191

It's crazy clothes that maketh personkind

IN THE fourteenth century women's fashion produced dresses which were so tight round the hips that their "mound of Venus" stood out for all to see, while their breasts were laced so high inside their low-necked dresses that "a candle could be stood upon them".

Medieval men, on the other hand, wore short coats specially designed to reveal their genitals, which were tucked into a very prominent, glovelike container called a braguette. Even clergymen wore such short frocks that "they did not cover the middle parts" – leaving their genitals exposed in tight stockings for all to admire. When all this was curbed, during the reign of Edward IV, lords and royalty were exempt, for the Commons petitioned only that "no knight, under the estate of a Lord ... nor any other person, use or wear ... any Gowne, jaket, or Cloke, but it be of such a length as it, he being upright, shall cover his privy members and buttokkes".

Button up!

Why do men and women wear buttons on opposite sides? At first, all buttons were worn on the left-hand side, but when coats became fashionable, men found they could not get hold of their swords quickly. To keep the sword hand free, buttons were placed on the right of the opening so they could be easily undone by the left hand.

"WHY THE LOOK OF SUPRISE, GEORGE — I TOLD YOU I HAD NOTHING TO WEAR!"

"FRANKLY, I DON'T THINK THE ABBOT'S GOING TO BE TOO WILD ABOUT YOUR DENIM!"

"IF THIS SHRINK DOES'NT COME UP WITH SOMETHING, WE'LL BE CALLING THE GODFATHER GODMOTHER!"

His Masterpiece

by 'Banjo' Paterson

GREENHIDE BILLY was a stockman on a Clarence River cattle-station and admittedly the biggest liar in the district. He had been for many years pioneering in the Northern Territory, the other side of the sun-down-a regular "furthest-out man" – and this assured his reputation among station-hands who award rank according to amount of experience.

Young men who have always hung around the home districts, doing a job of shearing here or a turn at horse-breaking there, look with reverence on Riverine or Macquarie-River shearers who come in with tales of runs where they have 300,000 acres of freehold land and shear

250,000 sheep; these again pale their ineffectual fires before the glory of the Northern Territory man who has all-comers on toast, because no one can contradict him or check his figures. When two of them meet, however, they are not fools enough to cut down quotations and spoil the market; they lie in support of each other, and make all other bushmen feel mean and pitiful and inexperienced.

Sometimes a youngster would timidly ask Greenhide Billy about the terra incognita: "What sort of a place is it, Billy-how big are the properties? How many acres had you in the place you were on?"

"Acres be d—d!" Billy would scornfully reply; "hear him talking about acres! D'ye think we were blanked cockatoo selectors! Out there we reckon country by the hundred miles. You orter say, 'How many thousand miles of country?' and then I'd understand you."

Furthermore, according to Billy, they reckoned the rainfall in the Territory by yards, not inches. He had seen blackfellows who could jump at least three inches higher than anyone else had ever seen a blackfellow jump, and every bushman has seen or personally known a blackfellow who could jump over six feet. Billy had seen bigger droughts, better country, fatter cattle, faster horses, and cleverer dogs, than any other man on the Clarence River. But one night when the rain was on the roof, and the river was rising with a moaning sound, and the men were gathered round the fire in the hut smoking and staring at the coals, Billy turned himself loose and gave us his masterpiece.

"I was drovin' with cattle from Mungrybanbone to old Corlett's station on the Buckadowntown River" (Billy always started his stories with some paralysing bush names). "We had a thousand head of store-cattle, wild, mountainbred wretches that'd charge you on sight; they were that handy with their horns they could skewer a mosquito. There was one or two one-eyed cattle among 'em-and you know how a one-eyed beast always keeps movin' away from the mob, pokin' away out to the edge of them so as they won't git on his blind side, so that by stirrin' about he keeps the others restless.

"They had been scared once or twice, and stampeded' and gave us all we could do to keep them together; and it was wet and dark and thundering, and it looked like a real bad night for us. It was my watch. I was on one side of the cattle, like it might be here, with a small bit of a fire; and my mate Barcoo Jim, he was right opposite on the other side of the cattle, and had gone to sleep under a log. The rest of the men were in the camp fast asleep. Every now and again I'd get on my horse and prowl round the cattle quiet like, and they seemed to be settled down all right, and I was sitting by my fire holding my horse and drowsing, when all of a sudden a blessed 'possum ran out from some saplings and scratched up a tree right alongside me. I was half-asleep, I suppose, and I was startled; anyhow, never thinking what I was doing, I picked up a firestick out of the fire and flung it at the 'possum.

"Whoop! Before you could say Jack Robertson, that thousand head of cattle were on their feet, and made one wild, headlong, mad rush right over the place where poor-old Barcoo Jim was sleeping. There was no time to hunt up materials for the inquest; I had to keep those cattle together, so I sprang into the saddle, dashed the spurs into the old horse, dropped my head on his mane, and sent him hard as he could leg it through the scrub to get to the lead of the cattle and steady them. It was brigalow, and you know what that is.

"You know how the brigalow grows," continued Bill;

"saplings about as thick as a man's arm, and that close together a dog can't open his mouth to bark in 'em. Well, those cattle were swept through that scrub, levelling it like as if it had been cleared for a railway line. They cleared a track a quarter of a mile wide, and smashed every stick, stump and sapling on it. You could hear them roaring and their hoofs thundering and the scrub smashing three or four miles off.

"And where was I? I was racing parallel with the cattle, with my head down on the horse's neck, letting him pick his way through the scrub in the pitchy darkness. This went on for about four miles. Then the cattle began to get winded, and I dug into the old stock-horse with the spurs, and got in front, and began to crack the whip and sing out, so as to steady them a little; after awhile they dropped slower and slower, and I kept the whip going. I got them all together in a patch of open country, and there I rode round and round 'em all night till daylight.

"And how I wasn't killed in the scrub, goodness only knows; for a man couldn't ride in the daylight where I did in the dark. The cattle were all knocked about – horns smashed, legs broken, ribs torn; but they were all there, every solitary head of 'em; and as soon as the daylight broke I took 'em back to the camp – that is, all that could travel, because I had to leave a few broken-legged ones."

Billy paused in his narrative. He knew that some suggestions would be made, by way of compromise, to tone down the awful strength of the yarn, and he prepared himself accordingly. His motto was "No surrender;" he never abated one jot of his statements; if anyone chose to remark on them, he made them warmer and stronger, and absolutely flattened out the intruder.

"That was a wonderful bit of ridin' you done, Billy," said

one of the men at last, admiringly. "It's a wonder you wasn't killed. I suppose your clothes was pretty well tore off your back with the scrub?"

"Never touched a twig," said Billy. "Ah!" faltered the inquirer, "then no doubt you had a real ringin' good stock-horse that could take you through a scrub like that full-split in the dark, and not hit you against anything."

"No, he wasn't a good un," said Billy decisively, "he was the worst horse in the camp. Terrible awkward in the scrub he was, always fallin' down on his knees; and his neck was so short you could sit far back on him and pull his ears."

Here that interrogator retired hurt; he gave Billy best. After a pause another took up the running.

"How did your mate get on, Billy? I s'pose he was trampled to a mummy!"

"No," said Billy, "he wasn't hurt a bit. I told you he was sleeping under the shelter of a log. Well, when those cattle rushed they swept over that log a thousand strong; and every beast of that herd took the log in his stride and just missed landing on Barcoo Jimmy by about four inches."

The men waited a while and smoked, to let this statement soak well into their systems; at last one rallied and had a final try.

"It's a wonder then, Billy," he said, "that your mate didn't come after you and give you a hand to steady the cattle."

"Well, perhaps it was," said Billy, "only that there was a bigger wonder than that at the back of it."

"What was that?"

"My mate never woke up all through it."

Then the men knocked the ashes out of their pipes and went to bed. #

SHADY CHARACTERS

How to play

Unscramble five Australian prime ministers to make a sixth in the shaded column.

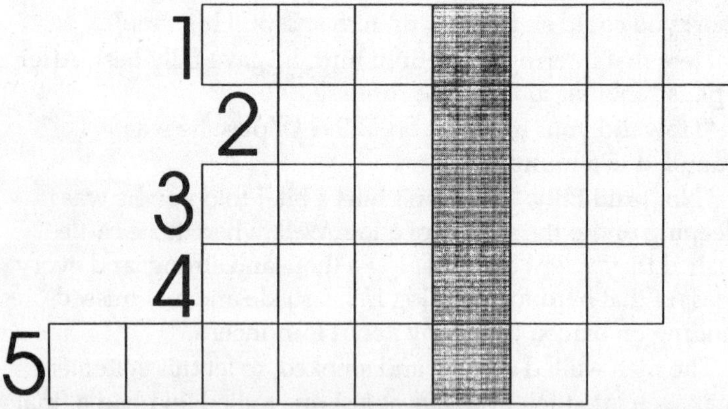

1. **SHRIFE**
2. **ARREFS**
3. **NEWCEM**
4. **AKEDIN**
5. **SIZEMEN**

Answers on Page 191

Pardon me, but exactly what do you mean?

TO A FOREIGNER, everyday English literally translated is often quite incomprehensible. Everyone knows, for instance, that blood is red – yet we commonly talk of people with blue blood. Others are said to weep crocodile tears, or go around with a chip on the shoulder, lose their face, or enjoy the hair of a dog.

But how, literally, can you steal someone's thunder, be on tenterhooks, eat humble pie, feel down in the dumps, get short shrift, or buy a white elephant at the corner store? What is your Nellie? And who was the Real McCoy – or Hobson whose choice is still no choice at all?

All, of course, are idiomatic expressions which say something quite different from their literal meaning. But just how did that happen? Here are some of the amazing origins of some of our most common idioms.

Acid test: Gold reacts to certain acids, which are used to test it for purity. The mixture of nitric acid and hydrochloric acid is called Aqua Regia (Latin for 'royal water') because it dissolves gold, considered the most noble metal.

Albatross around someone's neck: In Samuel Taylor Coleridge's poem *Rime of the Ancient Mariner* (1798), a sailor shoots an albatross, bringing bad luck to the ship. As punishment, his shipmates hang the dead bird around his neck and although it physically drops off when he repents, his guilt continues to haunt him.

Apple of the eye: In Deuteronomy, the Bible tells how the Lord protected Jacob as "the apple of his eye". This phrase for a treasured possession comes from the old-fashioned belief that a pupil of the eye is round, hard and shiny like an apple.

Axe to grind: Benjamin Franklin is best known as the scientist who invented the lightning conductor and as one of the authors of the American Declaration of Independence. Yet anyone with an axe to grind owes him a word of thanks. As a young boy Franklin, while turning his father's grindstone, was approached by a man too lazy to sharpen his own axe. He asked Franklin to explain how a grindstone worked, offering his own axe for use. He kept on praising the boy's ability to operate such an intricate machine until his axe had been sharpened – then laughed as he walked away.

Bald as a coot: The coot, a common water bird around 40cm long, has a white bill which extends to its forehead, giving an appearance of baldness when viewed against the dark plumage. The idiom goes back at least to the 15th Century. See also **Crazy as a coot**

Battle royal: Today meaning a general squabble, the phrase did not, as many people suppose, originate in the days when kings and noble knights clashed in hand-to-hand combat. It was used in cockfighting to describe a contest in which a number of cocks were pitted against each other until one emerged victorious from the battle royal.

Beard the lion in his den: Used idiomatically to describe a face-to-face confrontation, the phrase was coined by Sir Walter

"JUST IN CASE OUR PRAYERS AREN'T ANSWERED
- DO WE HAVE ANYONE IN OUR MIDST
EXPERIENCED IN LION TAMING ?"
JACKSON-GRAHAM

Scott in his 1808 poem *Marmion*:

And dar'st thou then
Beard the lion in his den. ?

Beer money: English soldiers traditionally received a ration of beer each day, the equivalent of the naval tot of rum or grog (watered down rum). Between 1800 and 1823 they were given an allowance of a penny a day beer money instead, which eventually became synonymous with money to be spent on pleasure.

The best laid plans of mice and men: By implication, they usually go wrong, as Robert Burns (1759-96) points out in "To a Mouse", leaving us "...nought but grief an' pain/For promis'd joy"

Blue blood: Othello, Shakespeare's famous Moor, certainly had no blue blood: his skin was much to dark for that. The phrase originated with noble Spanish families who prided themselves on having skins so white that every blue vein could be clearly seen – a sure sign that they had no Moorish blood.

Bury the hatchet: Before American Red Indians smoked the peace pipe, they buried hatchets, knives, clubs and other weapons so that no indications of war would be visible.

To cast the first stone: Commonly applied to persons who are quick to criticize, the idiom started out as a biblical warning that no one is completely faultless. When Jesus came across a crowd who wanted to stone to death an adultress, he warned them: "He that is without sin among you, let him cast the first stone at her." No one did.

Chip on his shoulder: Last century an American youth determined to prove his toughness would put a chip of wood on his shoulder, then fight anyone who dared knock it off.

Climb on the bandwagon: In the United States and some other countries years ago it was traditional for a band, playing on a wagon, to escort a political candidate through the town. By climbing on the bandwagon, local leaders would openly declare their support for the candidate.

Crazy as a coot: These common water birds congregate in large numbers in winter, squabbling noisily for no obvious reason – which makes them appear somewhat demented. The idiom "silly old coot" probably has the same origin.

Crocodile tears: Crocodiles, it was once believed, lured victims to river banks by making noises like a person in trouble. The charade continued even after the reptile had caught its prey, for it was said the beast would weep hypocritically while enjoying its meal. Noted the Elizabethan statesman and philosopher, Sir Francis Bacon: 'It is the wisdom of the crocodiles, that shed tears when they would devour.'

'IF THAT WAS A DOG HE'D BRING MY WALKING STICK BACK!!'

Dead as a dodo: This idiom for something extinct or out of fashion was inspired by the dodo, a flightless bird similar in size to a turkey, that was last observed in Mauritius in the 1680s.

Dead as a doornail: The nail in this idiom – which has been traced back to as early as 1350 – is thought to be the striking plate of a doorknocker which is bashed on the "head" every time a visitor arrives.

Dead ringer for: A horse falsely entered to run a race in place of another it resembles is known as a "ringer" Today the term means anything or anyone closely resembling another.

Devil to pay: Today generally meaning trouble ahead, the complete idiom – "The Devil to pay and no pitch hot" – originated in the days of sailing ships. When caulking a wooden ship, one of the most difficult seams to cover (or "pay") with tar was the one near the keel, known to sailors as the "devil" If that was not done quickly with hot pitch before the tide came in, the ship could be in trouble.

Don Juan: Still the symbol of a seducer in the "love-her-and-leave-her" mould, the original Don Juan Tenorio was born in Seville in the 14th Century and is credited (in Mozart's opera *Don Giovanni*) with having more than 2500 mistresses.

" WHEN WILL YOU GET IT INTO YOUR HEAD, HENDERSON ? – YOU'RE A PUBLIC RELATIONS MAN, NOT A PUBLIC CONVENIENCE !!

Down in the dumps: Any musician worth his salt (Roman soldiers were paid in salt, which was translated into English as salary) should be able to play the dumps. This obsolete English word once described a sad or plaintive piece of music – which left listeners of old feeling decidedly down.

Enough to make the angels weep: For this apt description of very foolish behaviour we are indebted to Shakespeare's *Measure for Measure*: "...But man, proud man,/Dress'd in a little brief authority,/...Plays such fantastic tricks before high heaven/As make the angels weep".

Feather in your cap: American Indians had to kill at least one enemy before they could decorate their headdress with a feather – and each additional victim entitled them to add another feather. The custom of using feathers to denote bravery and as a mark of distinction has been widespread for centuries in other parts of the world as well.

Fifth column: Referring to traitors working secretly for the enemy, the expression comes from a radio speech delivered during the Spanish Civil War by General Emilio Mola (1887-1937), who said he had four columns surrounding Madrid and a fifth column already at work inside the city.

Fools rush in where angels fear to tread: Used to describe hasty action by inexperienced people, the idiom derives from Alexander Pope's *An Essay on Criticism* (1711).

Fourth Estate: Referring to the Press (actually the reporters' gallery in the British House of Commons) author Thomas Babington Macauley in 1828 named it the Fourth Estate. Traditionally the first three English "estates" were the Lords Spiritual (the Church), the Lords Temporal (the nobility) and the Commons.

STOP PRESS!

He was reported to have a broken nose, broken or chipped ribs and a fractured hand.

But violence and injury are not new to Mr Urquhart, who is married with three children and has a home in

DUKE OF GLOUCESTER

The Duke of Gloucester is suffering from a slight chill and is confined to his room at Barnwell Manor, Northamptonshire. He was unable to attend the golden jubilee dinner of the Institute of Refrigeration in London last night.

BEAMING MR. K

After the dinner Mr. Khruschev led Mrs. Eisenhower by the arm down the Embassy steps, while President Eisenhower took Mrs. Khruschev's ars. The Soviet Prime Minister was smiling broadly and obviously enjoying himself.

Aiming High

The clergy witnessed the rehearsal and broadcast of this and of the daily service at home. The actual broadcast of both was a revelation, and a wonderful example of recollected concentration, preparation and what must be called team-work at its best. Nor will anyone forget the delicious touch when George Thalben Ball walked in and promptly pushed his organ round till he got it in the right place. Then he accompanied the service superbly.

MAIL ORDER CIGARETTES
SAVE $$$s — SEND A S.A.E.
FOR A FULL PRICE LIST
QUEENSLAND TOBACCO
P.O. BOX 5456
1 SPINAKER COURT,
CURRUMBIN WATERS, QLD. 4223
WARNING — SMOKING IS A HEALTH HAZARD (QLD. EXCEPTED)

He told Mrs. X he had a record of the complete works of the Messiah and she arranged to visit his house the next day to hear it.

"I was playing the Messiah for about 10 minutes when she said this was not the right occasion for such music," Ebbe went on. "She started to make overtures to me."

She told him to stop play

He was arrested and became violent assaulting a police officer.

After being placed in a police vehicle, he was subjected to a breast test which proved positive.

He was charged with mid-range PCA, refuse breath test

Get off scot free: Replace "scot" with its modern equivalent "payment" and it's obvious why the idiom refers to someone who escapes a debt or obligation.

Gift of the gab: In old Gaelic word "gab" meant "mouth" (still found today in the expression **shut your gob**), so the idiom refers to someone with the ability to speak easily and fluently.

Gild the lily: "To gild refined gold, to paint the lily,/ ... is wasteful and ridiculous excess," says Shakespeare in *King John* of the monarch who attempted to "improve" his royalty by having himself crowned a second time. Gold, already the purest of metals, cannot be improved by gilt; nor can the lily, symbol in Christian art of purity, be made more perfect by paint. As time made the phrase an English idiom, it became corrupted so that the lily, not the gold, was being gilded when someone attempted to make something already good appear to be even better.

Give short shrift: Before complaining that you've been given short shrift by someone, thank your lucky stars it's not really the case. Originally the term referred to the short few minutes allowed a priest to hear the confession of a criminal who was about to be executed.

Ham actor: There are many theories about the origin of this phrase to describe an amateurish, inferior actor (or actress). The most likely source is Shakespeare's *Hamlet,* where in Act III scene 2 Hamlet instructs a travelling band of players on how to avoid bad acting: "...do not saw the air too much with your hand," or "tear a passion to tatters, to very rags..." In most texts, Hamlet is abbreviated to "Ham".

LADDER WORDS

Write the word that fits the first clue into space 1 Drop one letter and rearrange to form the answer to clue 2. Drop one more letter, rearrange and get the answer to clue 3. Put the first dropped letter into the box to the left of space 1 and the other dropped letter into the box right of space 3. Continue in this fashion and when you have completed the puzzle, the dropped letters in the boxes on the left and right, when read down, will name a past prime minister of Australia.

A	1 FEARED	2 FREED	3 DEER	F
	4	5	6	
	7	8	9	
	10	11	12	
	13	14	15	
	16	17	18	

CLUES

1. *DREADED*
2. *RELEASED*
3. *ANTLERED ANIMAL*
4. *PART OF THE FOOT*
5. *MALICE*
6. *FAVOURITES*
7. *HORSE RIDER'S SEAT*
8. *DISTRIBUTES CARDS*
9. *GO FIRST*
10. *EXTEND*
11. *PAIN*
12. *DISTINGUISHED AIRMAN*
13. *BE AGREEABLE*
14. *SLIP OF MEMORY*
15. *MATES*
16. *CORRESPOND*
17. *LAYER*
18. *FASTEN WITH STRING*

Answers on Page 191

What a weird way to go!

THE ATHENIAN politician Draco was so popular that he was literally killed by kindness – giving rise to the popular expression we still use today. In 590 BC, after delivering a rousing speech in the theatre of Aegina, the spectators expressed their admiration by showering Draco with so many caps and cloaks that they suffocated him.

Sunday, bloody Sunday

Sunday is the most dangerous day for English kings and queens. Since 1066, seven have died on that day. Monday, Tuesday and Thursday have seen the end of six sovereigns each, Wednesday and Friday of five, and Saturday of four.

Onward Christian martyrs

Legend has it that St Peter was crucified (at his own request, upside down because he did not consider himself worthy of dying in the same way as Jesus) in Rome in AD 65. How did the other Apostles die? Most of them horribly, if church tradition is anything to go by.

Andrew was crucified on an X-shaped cross, Bartholomew was flayed with a knife. Two were bashed to death: James the Less with a heavy pole, Jude with a club. Matthew and Matthias were beheaded with axes. (A sword allegedly used to cut off the head of St Paul is kept at the convent of La Lisla in Spain.) Simon was sawn into pieces, while Thomas was killed by a lance. Philip was hanged from a tall pillar.

"THAT'S WHAT I CALL A BORN OPTIMIST!"

Strange deaths of famous people

Aeschylus, father of Greek drama, was killed in 456 BC by a tortoise dropped on his bald head by an eagle! The bird, keen to break the shell, had apparently mistaken the shiny dome for a stone.

Experimenting with refrigeration, the philosopher Francis Bacon was stuffing a chicken with snow in 1626 when he caught a cold – which killed him.

King Edward IV forced his brother George, Duke of Clarence, to drink himself to death – literally. He had George put to death in the Tower of London in 1478 by drowning him in a tub of sweet Malmsey wine.

Yellow peril

Who needs the Bomb? One statistician has calculated that if all the Chinese jumped into the air and hit the ground together, the shock would create a tidal wave that would engulf most of the United States.

No flies on him

Pope Adrian VI choked to death – on a fly which flew into his throat as he was taking a drink of water.

Headstrong wife

When Sir Walter Raleigh was beheaded in 1618, his widow had his head embalmed and placed in a leather bag, which she carried with her everywhere until her death 29 years later.

Food for thought

French poet William de Cabestan made a mistake when he vied with chef Raymond de Seillans for the love of a maiden. The chef not only murdered poor Willy, but cut out his heart and served it to the lady – who died from shock when she discovered what she was eating.

Dying

'I DON'T BELIEVE IT! – I WAS KNITTING THIS SWEATER FOR HIM ...'

'AND NOW THE INSCRIPTION ... A NICE TOUCH DON'T YOU THINK?'

'HE WAS'NT A BAD ACTOR, BUT I SAID TO HIM TIME AND TIME AGAIN, NEVER PERFORM WITH CHILDREN AND ANIMALS!

"WHAT'S THE BETTING THAT LIFE INSURANCE COMPANY WE'RE PAYING INTO CALLS THIS, AN ACT OF THE GODS?"

"HOW DID YOUR SWORD FIGHTING CLASS GO, DEAR ?"

"THE ONE IN THE MIDDLE WAS THE GAME WARDEN!

AUSTRALIA'S PAST

1 Captain (later Sir) Neville Howse was the first Australian to win a Victoria Cross, for his heroism during the war in (a) Sudan; (b) Gallipoli; (c) South Africa; (d) New Guinea.

2 Parliament House in Canberra was opened by the Duke of York on 2 May (a) 1912; (b) 1919; (c) 1927; (d) 1931.

3 When Lieutenant (later Sir) Ross Smith and his crew landed their Vickers Vimy aircraft at Darwin on December 10, 1919, they won a £10,000 prize as the first aviators to fly to Australia in under 30 days from (a) Canada; (b) England; (c) India; (d) the United States.

4 The member of the New Guard who used a sword to cut the ribbon at the opening of the Sydney Harbour Bridge was Captain (a) John Lang; (b) Isaac Isaacs; (c) Philip Game; (d) F.E. De Groot.

5 The celebrated Aboriginal landscape painter Albert Namatjira was sentenced to jail in 1958 for (a) murder; (b) supplying liquor to fellow Aborigines; (c) theft; (d) forgery.

6 Australia's first telephone exchange opened in August 1880 in (a) Sydney; (b) Geelong; (c) Melbourne; (d) Ballarat.

7 The first colony to have its own flag - when in 1856 it became the first to acquire a warship - was (a) SA; (b) Vic; (c) NSW; (d) Ql.

8 On March 18, 1910, the famous escapologist Harry Houdini (real name Ehrich Weiss) distinguished himself at Diggers Rest, Victoria, when he (a) escaped from a coffin 30 metres under water; (b) ascended 858 metres in a hot-air balloon; (c) performed Australia's first controlled powered flight in a Voisin biplane; (d) won the world heavyweight wrestling title.

9 The Northern Territory of South Australia was taken over by the Commonwealth at a ceremony in Palmerston (as Darwin was then known) on January 2, (a) 1869; (b) 1899; (c) 1911; (d) 1928.

10 The second Christian name of Sir Robert Menzies, who retired in

1966 after a total of almost 19 years as Prime Minister, was (a) Gordon; (b) George; (c) Gisborne; (d) Gabriel.

11 The sailing ship *Hougoumont* on January 9, 1868 landed the last convicts transported to Australia at (a) Brisbane; (b) Launceston; (c) Fremantle; (d) Port Adelaide.

12 Kenyon St Vincent Welsh, the first Flying Doctor, introduced the outback medical service in May 1928 from (a) Mount Isa; (b) Cloncurry; (c) Darwin; (d) Port Augusta.

13 Australia's first bank, which opened on April 8, 1817, was (a) Bank of New South Wales (now Westpac); (b) Bank of Australia; (c) Van Diemen's Land Bank Co.; (d) Commercial Bank of Australasia.

14 Women were given the vote for the first time in Australia in December 1894 with the passing of the Adult Suffrage Bill in (a) Queensland; (b) Victoria; (c) South Australia; (d) Western Australia.

15 Australia's oldest university, established in 1850, is the University of (a) Queensland; (b) Sydney; (c) New South Wales; (d) Adelaide.

16 The last full-blood survivor of the Tasmanian Aborigines, who died in 1876 at the age of 73, was named (a) King Billy; (b) Truganini; (c) Pullabooka; (d) Queenie.

17 The code name "Anzac" was first adopted for the Australian and New Zealand Army Corps during WWI while they were stationed in (a) Palestine; (b) Egypt; (c) the Dardanelles; (d) the Somme.

18 The first Commonwealth postage stamps, which replaced stamps issued by various State governments, were introduced in (a) 1901; (b) 1910; (c) 1923; (d) 1934.

19 The Christian names of J.P. Fawkner, the convict's son who became one of the founders of Melbourne, was (a) John Pascoe; (b) John Peter; (c) John Percival; (d) John Pessimist.

20 Three unions merged in 1972 to form Australia's largest trade union, the (a) Builders' Labourers Federation; (b) Miners' Federation; (c) Waterside Workers' Federation; (d) Amalgamated Metal Workers' Union.

Answers on Page 191

SHADY CHARACTERS

How to play

Unscramble these five fish to make a sixth in the shaded column.

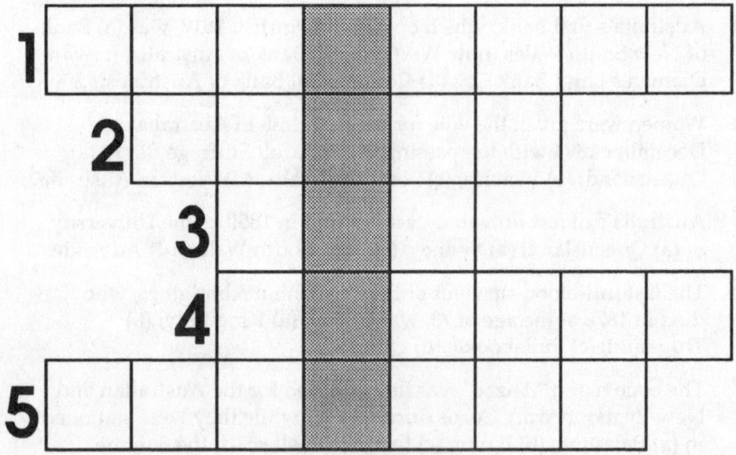

CLUES

1. **HEADLAFT**
2. **PHREC**
3. **DOC**
4. **LUMTEL**
5. **THWINGI**

Answers on Page 191

The long and the short and the tall

UP TO the 18th century dwarfs were found in many of Europe's royal households. The last dwarf at the English Court was Coppernin, the human pet of the mother of King George III. In Russia dwarfs were so highly prized that one miniature couple in 1710 received a royal invitation to spend their wedding night in the bedchamber of the Czar. The smallest dwarf on record was named, appropriately, the Fairy Queen. When exhibited in London in 1850, she stood a mere 40.64cm tall on feet less than 5cm long.

Top that!

James Heatherington caused consternation when he wore his latest invention – the top hat – in London on 5 January 1797. So great was the outcry that he was taken before the Lord Mayor and charged with appearing "on a public highway wearing upon his head a tall structure having a shining lustre and calculated to frighten timid people". He was found guilty and bound over to keep the peace.

Goliath still tops

The Bible tells us that Goliath, the most famous giant in history, stood somewhere between 2.97 metres and 3.43 metres tall. No one in recent history has come anywhere near that. The tallest person measured scientifically this century was Robert Pershing Wadlow, born in 1918 in the United States. At the age of 14 he towered 2.26 metres above the ground; when he died in 1940 he was 2.72 metres tall.

"HE'S A GREAT BELIEVER IN ALTERNATE MEDICINE, DOCTOR — WHISKY!"

How nosy can you get?

The world's longest known nose, which belonged to Thomas Wedders, an 18th Century Englishman, protruded 19.05 cm. It was reported to be very red.

O, Feathers!

The longest surname in everyday use in Britain and Australia is Featherstonehaugh. The shortest is O, a name often found in Korea.

The Ben in Big Ben

Big Ben is perhaps London's most famous landmark – but strictly speaking the name refers not to the clock but only to the 13.5 tonne bell in St Stephen's Tower of the Houses of Parliament. It was named after Sir Benjamin Hall, Chief Commissioner of Works in 1856 when the famous bell was cast. Hall's nickname? Big Ben – because of his size.

Stand back, boys

Who's the biggest: man or woman? When it comes to cells, females win easily. The ovum, or egg, is the largest cell in the human body, while the sperm cell is the smallest.

Big noise, indeed

Just how large – and loud – is the world's largest musical instrument? The Auditorium Organ, built in Atlantic City, USA, in 1930, has two consoles, 1477 stop controls, and 33,122 pipes, ranging in size from 4.7 mm to 19 metres. It makes as much noise as seven brass bands!

Permanent leap year?

If a man, in proportion to his weight, could jump as high as a flea, he could clear the tallest church tower with ease.

TOUGH ONE

HOW TO PLAY

Using all the letters below (only once) form five 5-letter words, adding the letter "T" twice in each word.

AA	**1.**	_ _ _ _ _
C		
EEE	**2.**	_ _ _ _ _
II		
K	**3.**	_ _ _ _ _
M		
P	**4.**	_ _ _ _ _
SS		
YY	**5.**	_ _ _ _ _

Answers on Page 191

Superstitious? Not me (touch wood)!

MANY punters at Sydney racetracks say it's bad luck to light a cigarette while a race is in progress. Also taboo are carrying copper coins, wearing green on the track, or turning back to fetch something you had forgotten on the way to the track.

Sneaky spirits

Exorcists believe that once devils and evil spirits have been driven out of the body, they will try everything possible to regain entry. At the end of a Catholic exorcism ceremony, the nine openings of the body are sprinkled with holy water to "seal" them against re-entry. All meals and drinks are also blessed in advance to prevent spirits sneaking in that way.

Go fly a kite

When last did you go fly a kite? According to Chinese custom, its the ideal way to clear your conscience. Teng Kao (Feast of High Flight), which is celebrated on the ninth day of the ninth month of the Chinese year, attracts millions of kiteflyers. At the end of the day, the kites are cut loose – each carrying away with it the bad deeds the flyer committed during the previous year.

Love diet

Want to lose weight? Then get romantic! According to researchers, an average "romantic interlude" rids you of three hundred calories, while a passionate kiss accounts for twelve.

A Scandinavian woman once filed a paternity suit against Uri Geller because she claimed that he had uncoiled her copper IUD during one of his mind-bending exercises.

Crazy about love

Kinsey's statistics on male sexual behaviour reveal that persons who abstain from sex are more likely to suffer mental instability than those who do not.

Heaven forbid!

At least twelve churches boast the foreskin of Jesus Christ, removed through circumcision, among their sacred relics – among them Antwerp, Coulombs, Charroux, Hildesheim, Puy-en-Velay and St. John Lateran.

And while on the subject of the Church and sex: medieval Catholic philosopher St Thomas Aquinas held that masturbation was a greater sin than fornication.

Strange beliefs

Saying "white rabbits" and knocking on wood at the beginning of the month is said to bring money from an unexpected source. "If I forget, no money," a woman from Gosford, New South Wales, told a newspaper a few years ago. "Try it, it always works for me."

"YOU CAN TAKE OFF THAT GARLIC NECKLACE — MOTHER ISN'T COMING!"

Sir Robert Helpman, Australia's internationally known dancer and choreographer, has as his lucky talisman a black braid tie given to him by Manoletti, the famous bullfighter. While he wears it, everything will be well, Sir Robert believes.

Superstitious residents in the Darling River region of New South Wales claimed the Darling pea had magical powers. Anyone who picked the beautiful flower, it was widely believed, would not leave the region for seven years. The same belief in some areas also applied to the Darling lily. Bushmen claimed horses eating the Darling pea became mad.

Australian settlers and convicts early last century believed a person or animal bitten by a snake would die at around sunset.

Wattle blossoms brought into a house brings bad luck, it is widely believed in many parts of Australia.

WORD BUILDING

COUNTRIES

Begin with the first word in column "A", then select a word from column "B"and then one from column "C", in that order, so that three small words form one large word. All answers are names of countries.

	A	B	C
1	GRE	GAP	LIA
2	AUS	ZIL	AND
3	SIN	ENL	ORE
4	SWA	TRA	AND

1. ____________________
2. ____________________
3. ____________________
4. ____________________

Answers on Page 191

Oddly Australian!

AUSTRALIA, home to such unique animals as the kangaroo and the wombat, is an odd continent by any standards. But not only because of nature: Australians have created some amazing (and very amusing) oddities in the 200-odd years of living on the world's largest island. Here are some of them:

Anvils

At Dunolly, Victoria, a rusting old anvil in front of the historical museum commemorates the destruction of the world's largest gold nugget, the "Welcome Stranger".

Discovered by John Deason and Richard Oates under only 2cm of gravel at Moliagul, near Dunolly, on 5 January 1869, the 71,040 gram nugget was cut into smaller pieces on the anvil at Dunolly early the following month. This reduced what could have been one of the world's most sought-after collector's items into mere lumps of gold. A replica of the nugget is on display in the Dunolly historical centre. In February 1969 grandsons of the founders, also bearing the names Deason and Oates, re-enacted the finding of the nugget at Moliagul, where a simple obelisk now marks the site of the big find.

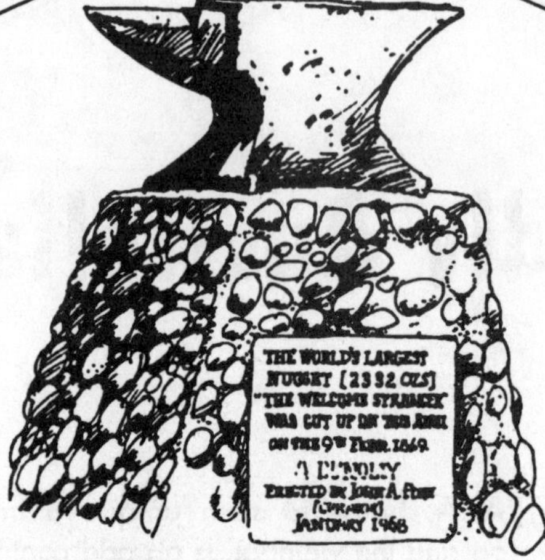

Dunolly Anvil, Victoria

The anvil on which Les Darcy, one of Australia's finest and most controversial boxers, developed some of the muscles which enabled him to punch his way to forty wins in forty-four fights, twenty by knock-out, can be seen at the Hunter Valley Museum of Rural Life, on the shores of Lake Glenbawn, 13km from Scone, New South Wales. The anvil is from the East Maitland forge where Darcy, at the age of sixteen, was apprenticed in 1911 before becoming a professional boxer.

ART

Never cross a priest who has an artist for a friend! That's the strange warning contained in the lavishly painted interior of St Mary's Catholic Church at Bairnsdale, Victoria.

In 1931 a jobless Italian migrant, Frank Floreani, asked the priest at St Mary's, Father Cremin, for permission to decorate his church. The priest agreed and for 6 shillings a day Floreani spent the next few years meticulously painting Biblical scenes on the walls and ceiling. The artist and the priest became good friends, but

Father Cremin had a badgering housekeeper who gave them both a hard time. So Floreani decided to teach her a lesson the entire congregation could not fail to notice – by painting her as the she-devil in a scene on the wall to the right of the altar. There she still is today, a warning to all of the power of the brush ...

Fairies Tree

FAIRY SANCTUARY

Australia's only fairy sanctuary is in Melbourne's Fitzroy Gardens, where exquisite portraits of many of these elusive creatures were carved on a tree by Ola Cohn, M.B.E., A.R.C.A., between 1931 and 1934. She did this as a gift to the children of the city, to whom she explained in her book, The Fairies' Tree, "I've carved a tree in the Fitzroy Gardens for you and the fairies, but mostly for the fairies, and those who believe in them, for they will understand how necessary it is to have a fairy sanctuary – a place that is sacred and safe as a home should be to all living creatures ..." The tree, in the heart of the gardens, is a favourite with children of all ages.

People's Arts path

ARTS PATH

Also in Fitzroy Gardens is a unique People's Arts Path, which was created in February 1978 by city residents who decorated more than 1000 ceramic tiles with highly individual designs. After glazing, the tiles were used to make a footpath in the north-east comer of the gardens.

BEDS

Australia abounds with relics of Ned Kelly. But perhaps one of the most unusual links with the infamous bushranger is housed in the historical museum at Mount Victoria, New South Wales – the bed of his sister, Kate. She was buried in 1898 at Forbes, in the State's central-west, after drowning.

The bed used by Mary, Queen of Scots in 1554, when she was twelve years old, can be seen at Winniston Park in Denmark, Western Australia. Also on display is what is claimed to be Australia's largest collection of sixteenthcentury English antiques.

BEER

The Northern Territory certainly takes its beer drinking seriously. Not only does it have the highest per capita beer consumption in the world – estimated at around 236 litres a year – but also boasts what is almost certainly the world's largest beer bottle, the "Eighty-ounce Darwin Stubby". Yet, despite this obvious predilection for liquor, Darwin's Society for the Prevention of Alcoholism was disbanded in 1966 "for lack of support"

BILLIARD TABLE

Swansea, Tasmania, claims to have Australia's only remaining billiard table weighing one tonne. It is housed in the town's 1860 Institute building, which now serves as a museum.

BRIDGE

Bendigo, Victoria, boasts a bridge so wide that the thousands who cross it daily never realise they have done so. In fact, at 200m, it is Australia's, and very likely the world's, widest bridge. It straddles Bendigo Creek at the bottom of View Street hill, where the creek flows underneath Charing Cross, the city's main intersection. Because of the surrounding built-up area, only the platform of the bridge can be seen, with no sign to indicate where it joins the banks of the creek on either side.

CASTLE

A medieval castle is the last thing you expect to see just outside Ballarat on the highway to Melbourne. Yet Kryal Castle is no mirage. Instead, it is a highly imaginative reconstruction of a sixteenth-century castle, built to satisfy the lifelong ambition of a local man, Keith Ryall. Now one of the main tourist attractions of

Kryal Castle

the former goldrush city, Kryal Castle has everything from a wooden drawbridge operated in medieval fashion, to replicas of the British Crown jewels valued at more than $100,000, a Bloody Tower, a scaffold featuring "hangings" several times a day, jousting tournaments, a magnificent weapons display, a wide range of torture instruments, and a variety of shops where craftsmen manufacture items using medieval methods. The castle was opened in November 1974.

CATHEDRALS

Probably Australia's most unusual place of worship is Green Cathedral at Tiona, 13km south of Forster, New South Wales. The open-air cathedral, on the shores of Lake Wallis, has a roof formed of tall palm trees and seats shaped from massive logs. It is used by the Reorganised Church of Jesus Christ of the Latter Day Saints.

The smallest cathedral in Australia is the Procathedral of St John the Baptist at Murray Bridge, South Australia. It was dedicated on 2 February 1887 and became the cathedral of the Bishop of the Murray in April 1970. Measuring 95.2 square metres and seating 130 people, it is only 1.6 square metres larger than the world's smallest cathedral, the Cathedral Chapel of St Francis at Laguna Beach, Florida, U.S.A., which was built in 1933 and can accommodate a congregation of only forty-two.

A miniature cathedral made of 20 948 pieces of marble – each piece cut and polished by hand – took Gundagai, New South Wales, artist Frank Rusconi twenty-eight years to construct in his spare time. It is now on display at the Gundagai Tourist Information Centre, Sheridan Street. Rusconi also sculpted the famous Dog on the Tuckerbox statue at Gundagai.

Old Watch House — smallest cell

CELL

The smallest solitary confinement cell ever used in Australia can still be seen at the Old Watch House on the Derwent River at Granton, Tasmania. It is 50cm square and 2m high. The Old Watch House was built by convicts in 1838 to guard the causeway across the river.

CENOTAPH

The world's only known replica, albeit on a smaller scale, of London's famous Whitehall Cenotaph is at Charing Cross in the heart of Bendigo, Victoria.

CHAIRS

The Battle of Trafalgar is commemorated in a most unusual way by two unusual and comfortable pieces of furniture in historic St Matthew's Church, which was built in 1843 in picturesque Rokeby, Tasmania. The intricately carved pair of chairs in the chancel were made of timber taken from one of the warships in Admiral Lord Nelson's victorious fleet.

Chair from wood of Nelson's ship

CHURCHES

A church with four foundation-stones can be seen in the small town of Yankalilla, South Australia. Now used by the Uniting Church, it was built in 1878 by members of the Bible Christian Methodist Church. The four foundationstones honour various church leaders. The Bible Christians amalgamated with the main body of the Methodist Church around the turn of the century.

St Peter's Church, on Lake Victoria at Paynesville, Victoria, is distinctly nautical, both inside and out. The spire is in the shape of a lighthouse tower, with a cross and a light which can be seen from far out on the Gippsland lakes. The pulpit represents the bow of a fishing boat, while the sanctuary light is modelled on a ship's riding light.

St Nicholas' Church at Australind, Western Australia, is almost certainly the smallest in the country, measuring a mere 7m by 4.06m. It was built around 1840 as a workman's cottage, but soon became a place of worship for Congregational settlers. The building was bought by the Church of England and blessed by Bishop Goldsmith on 23 December 1915. Services are still held there every Sunday morning.

Smallest Church in Aust.

CLOCKS

Why does the clock in the tower of Bendigo's main post office stop chiming at 11 o'clock each night? Because, it is claimed, when Dame Nellie Melba spent a few nights at the Shamrock Hotel, opposite the post office, well over half a century ago, she complained that the chiming disturbed her sleep. So the authorities obligingly silenced the clock at 11 p.m. – and never reset it.

Life-size figures of a father and his son appear each hour in the tower of the T&G Building in the heart of Geelong, Victoria. The farmer strikes the time on a bell, while symbolically handing over to the next generation and urging his son to carry on his work. The figures have on occasion been dressed in Geelong Australian Rules guernseys and even (on New Year's eve) in kilts. The clock was installed in 1934. The cast bronze figures, bell and base weigh about 5 tonnes.

Take a good look at the eastern face of the clock on the town hall of Gawler, South Australia. Notice anything odd? Think about it before you read on. Stumped? Well, this clock can never tell 6 o'clock, only 4 o'clock twice. A plaque on the wall of the town hall explains, "It is a feature of historic interest that the eastern face of the clock, which was placed in service on September 6, 1867, shows 'IV' where the numeral 'VI' should appear. It is believed that this error occurred during manufacture."

Gawler Town Hall Clock

Two diggers operating a gold-washing cradle, and claimed to be the largest animated figures on a clock in Australia, entertain the people of Stawell, Victoria, for 90 seconds on the hour each day. Their actions, symbolising the goldmining history of the area, are accompanied by Westminster chimes. The clock, on Stawell's town hall, also plays the folk tune "With my swag on my shoulder" at 2 minutes to the hour.

One of Australia's strangest and largest clocks survives in the heart of Semaphore, near Port Adelaide, South Australia. It is a time-ball tower with a tall mast, erected in 1875 to enable ships in the anchorage off Port Adelaide and in the inner harbour to rate their chronometers. A plaque on the building explains, 'The black ball was hoisted to the masthead at 12.57 p.m. daily and dropped at 1.00 p.m. by electric release from the Adelaide Observatory. With the advent of wireless time signals, the service was discontinued in 1932." Similar time-ball towers were once used at other Australian ports.

Semaphore Tower

CLUB

Probably the most bizarre club in Australia insists that members touch their drinking vessels only with their left hands – except on Wednesdays, when they are permitted to use only their right hands.

The Left Hand Club in Whyalla, South Australia, was established in 1942 to raise funds for war relief and for charity – which it did by imposing fines on members breaking any of the club rules. In addition to the left-hand/right-hand rule, which applies at all times, the club bans other practises between noon and 2 p.m., and 5 p.m. to 6 p.m. on specific days of the week.

Monday, for instance, is "No Borrow Day", when members may not ask for matches, cigarettes, or the time of day, nor in any way beg or ask a favour from fellow members. Tuesday is "Yes Day", when members may not use the words "Yes", "Yeah", or "Umm", nor nod the head indicating the affirmative when in the presence or company of other members. On Friday members may not use the word "No", or indicate the negative with a shake of the head. Those caught breaking the rules are fined a silver coin.

CURIOSITY SHOP

The Old Curiosity Shop in Ballarat, Victoria, is perhaps the strangest memorial a man ever left to himself. For fortythree years until his death in 1898, bricklayer James Warwick decorated almost every centimetre of his quaint home with an endless medley of objects, broken and whole, in a great variety of colours.

The many thousands of items cemented into the walls include teapot lids and spouts; dolls' heads, legs, arms, and bodies, including one in porcelain now worth

Curiosity Shop

around $2000; jugs; dishes; plaques; shells; rocks; bottles; broken glass; statuettes; ornaments, and so on. The inside of the house is wallpapered entirely from sample books of wallpaper, with little regard to matching colours. The house is crammed with a motley collection of valuables and curiosities.

It was given the name "Old Curiosity Shop", after the Dickens novel, by local children who received a small reward from Warwick for any items of interest they brought him.

DEATH MASKS

Ned Kelly Death Mask

The death masks of Ned Kelly and many other felons executed at the Old Melbourne Gaol are on display in a cell in the only surviving wing of the prison, which is now a National Trust museum. The prisoners' heads were cut off after execution, the hair and beards shaved, and a cast taken, which was used to make a plaster death mask of the entire head.

DRAGONS

Bendigo, Victoria, has the largest Imperial Chinese dragon in the world. Sun Loong, as the 90-metre-long embroidered silk dragon is known, is the star of the city's Easter fair, which has been held annually since 1871. The brightly coloured dragon was lengthened a few years ago when Melbourne tried to upstage Bendigo with a longer dragon. Sun Loong, who is more than eighty years old, plays a central part in the parade through the picturesque mining city. At the "Waking of the Dragon" ceremony, held during the fair, Sun Loong is roused by fireworks. Bendigo is one of only five dragon cities in the world outside mainland China – the others are San

Francisco, Taipei, Hong Kong, and Singapore. The city also boasts the world's only night dragon, Yar Loong, who was displayed in 1938 during a special ceremony.

FENCE

The dingo fence which encloses the sheep farming areas of Queensland stretches for more than 5500km, making it the longest fence in the world. The fence which protects South Australia's sheep from dingoes is 2225km long.

FIRE LOOKOUT

The giant Gloucester Tree, outside Pemberton, Western Australia, is the highest forest fire observation post in the world. The lookout cabin, built in 1947, is 61m up the towering karri, and is reached via 153 rungs set into the wood. It overlooks 650 square kilometres of forest, farms, and coastal sand dunes. The tree, thought to be about 300 years old, was so named after a visit by the Duke of Gloucester.

FLAGS

The tattered remains of the "Southern Cross" flag, the battle flag of the Eureka miners' uprising at Ballarat, Victoria, in 1854, can be seen at the Ballarat Art Gallery. It has a broad white cross on a blue background, with five white stars, one at each point of the cross and one in the centre, representing the Southern Cross. The flag was originally 3.6m by 2.4m in size.

Eureka Stockade Flag

GALLOWS

Anyone who doubts that thirteen is an unlucky number should visit the Old Gaol at Dubbo, New South Wales. Now a museum, the prime attraction is the gallows, which has thirteen steps. Situated in the courtyard of the gaol, the gallows was built in the 1870s and last used on 28 June 1904 to hang the murderer Ah Chick. For those really interested in the macabre, there is a room displaying various tools of the hangman's trade.

GRAVE MATTERS

One expects to see weird things in a cemetery, but it still comes as a surprise to find a billiard table, complete with cue and balls, doing duty as a tombstone.

The unusual marble table, with pockets which double as flower vases, is in the Melbourne General Cemetery above the grave of Walter Lindrum, O.B.E., founder and former president of the Sportsmen's Association of Australia.

Lindrum, who died in 1960, aged sixty-one, reigned supreme as world professional billiard champion for eighteen years after defeating Joe Davis in 1932. He retired unbeaten in 1950, after breaking most of the world billiard records. His best performance was a break of 4137 points in 2 hours and 55 minutes, which included

1295 nursery cannons. He is buried alongside his wife, Beryl Elaine, who died five years after him.

If you see a halo-like glow in the graveyard of the small town of Louth, New South Wales, at around sunset, don't be frightened! It comes from a 1.2-metre-high metal cross topping the elaborate headstone on the grave of Mary Mathews, who died in 1868. The cross was specially positioned to create the halo-like reflection, which can be seen from various parts of the Louth Common throughout the year. The headstone was erected by Mary's husband, Mr I.E. Mathews, who founded the town in 1859.

HANDPRINTS

The handprints in concrete of our top country music artists can be seen at the Hands of Fame Comer Stone in the heart of Tamworth, New South Wales. The artists, selected by the organisers of the Australasian Country Music Awards, include Slim Dusty, Tex Morton, Reg Lindsay, Joy McKean, Hank Williams, and Smokey Dawson.

Not far away, at Radio Centre on Goonoo Goonoo Road, is the Roll of Renown, which was unveiled by Tex Morton in January 1977 One artist's name is added to the roll each year during the National Country Music Awards weekend.

HOUSE

A "moat" filled with soil imported from Ireland surrounds Sydney's historic Vaucluse House – to keep out snakes! The house was built in the early 1800s by Sir Henry Browne Hayes (1762-1832), a wealthy former sheriff of County Cork who had been transported to New South Wales for kidnapping a Quaker heiress. Because of his fear of snakes, Hayes had a "moat" 1.8m wide and 60cm deep

Sons of Gwalia headframe

dug around the house, which he then filled with 500 barrels of soil specially imported from Ireland for the purpose. It is claimed that as an added precaution, the superstitious Irishman had the work done on St Patrick's Day.

HEADFRAME

The headframe of the Sons of Gwalia goldmine, near Leonora, Western Australia, is perhaps Australia's most direct link with a president of the United States. The frame was designed and built under the supervision of Herbert Clark Hoover, a young mining engineer who during 1898 served as the first manager of the isolated mine. Hoover later exchanged mining for politics and in 1929 became the thirty-first President of the United States.

HORSE MEMORIAL

A unique statue of a horse at Nhill, Victoria, not only stands as a monument to the faithful drought horses who helped to develop Australia – it also tells their story. The "Talking Horse", which is claimed to be the only memorial of its kind in the world, speaks a recorded message when fed a coin.

A plaque explains that horse lovers subscribed to the erection of the statue "as a token of remembrance for these magnificent animals who sweated and toiled so faithfully..."

MiNIATURE VILLAGES

In Melbourne's Fitzroy Gardens is a delightful miniature Tudor village, which was presented to the city by the people of Lambeth, England, in appreciation of gifts of food sent by Victorians to England during the food shortage following the Second World War.

Another miniature display of British buildings and gardens, including the thatched village of Cockington and Scotland's Braemar Castle, can be seen at Cockington Green, near Canberra.

Prince Leonard, Hutt River Province

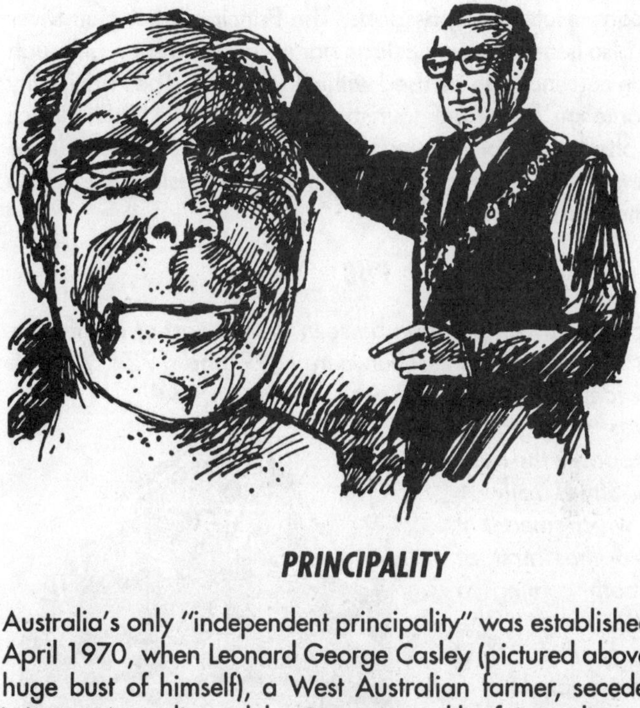

PRINCIPALITY

Australia's only "independent principality" was established on 21 April 1970, when Leonard George Casley (pictured above with a huge bust of himself), a West Australian farmer, seceded from Western Australia and the Commonwealth of Australia.

His 7486-hectare property became the Principality of Hutt River Province, ruled over by His Royal Highness Prince Leonard, Defender of the Faith, Protector of the Legends, Knight Grand Cross, the Most Noble Order of the Crusaders Cross of Jerusalem, Grand Officer of Ordre Chevalresque Nobiliaire et Religieux De La Couronne D'Epines, Sainte De Jerusalem, The Sovereign Military Teutonic Order, and Illustrious Cofradia De CabaBeros Cubiculario De La Real Order San Ildefonso.

Visitors need a visa to enter the Principality, which is situated 595km north of Perth, while Prince Leonard and his subjects – about thirty – carry Hutt River passports. The Principality of Hutt River Province also issues its own postage stamps and currency, although Australian currency can be used within its borders. The Principality has become an important tourist attraction, with H.R.H. Prince Leonard often personally issuing visas to visitors. The independence of the Principality is not recognised by either the Western Australian or Commonwealth governments.

PUB

Australia's narrowest pub can be seen in the heart of Kalgoorlie, where it did brisk business between 1899 and 1924. A mere 3.35m wide, the British Arms was strategically placed opposite the busy Hannan Street railway station, which meant it quenched the thirst of miners both coming to and leaving the fabulously rich West Australian goldfield.

After losing its liquor licence, the British Arms served as a boarding house until it was turned into the present Golden Mile Museum in 1968. Much of the rip-roaring history of the area is preserved there.

Narrowest Pub, Kalgoorlie

"Singing Ship"

SINGING SHIP

Ever heard a ship singing? If not, try Emu Park, near Yeppoon, Queensland, where a series of musical pipes fashioned into the shape of a ship "sing" whenever the wind blows. The singing ship is part of a monument at Churchill Lookout which commemorates the discovery of the Capricorn coast by Captain James Cook in May 1770. From the memorial can be seen all the islands and landmarks in Keppel Bay named by Cook.

SILVER TREE

A tree sculpted from 9kg of pure silver commemorates the discovery of the precious metal by Charles Rasp at Broken Hill in September 1883. Rasp commissioned an Adelaide silversmith, M. H. Steiner, to create the Silver Tree from the first silver mined at the site.

The tree is 864mm high and has a diameter of 406mm. Under the spreading branches are delicate figures of Aborigines, kangaroos, emus, sheep, and a lone boundary rider.

STREETS

Streets in the town of Southern Cross, Western Australia are all named after constellations and stars. The main street is named Antares Street, after the brightest star in the constellation of Scorpio and one of the largest known stars, while other names include Altair, Sirius, and Spica. The town was named by prospectors T. R. Risely and M. Toomey, who used the Southern Cross to guide them to a line of hills where they found gold in 1888.

Street names in Broken Hill, New South Wales reflect the Silver City's mining background. Most of the inner city streets are named after minerals and chemicals, such as Beryl, Crystal, Mica, Cobalt, Iodide, Oxide, Chloride, and Sulphide.

SUBMARINE

A replica of the small first World War submarine with which an Australian naval officer, N. D. Holbrook, torpedoed and sank a Turkish battleship in the Dardenelles in December 1914, can be seen in Holbrook, New South Wales. For this feat Holbrook, later a naval commander, became the first submariner to be awarded the Victoria Cross. Shortly afterwards the town Germanton was renamed Holbrook in his honour.

TOWN CENTRE

According to townsfolk, four corners in the heart of Ross, Tasmania, represent Temptation (Man o' Ross Hotel), Recreation (Town Hall), Salvation (church), and Damnation (gaol, now Council Chambers).

"TRAM - O TEL"

TRAMS

Lightning Ridge, the fascinating opal-mining town in the New South Wales outback, has a unique way of making Victorians feel at home. A number of old Melbourne trams, complete with route numbers and destination boards, have been converted to provide overnight accommodation as the country's only Tram-o-tel.

Bendigo, Victoria, operates a number of antique "talking trams", which give passengers a fascinating running commentary about the city, its buildings, and people. The tape-recorded commentary is synchronised by the tram driver to ensure that each building is discussed as the tram passes by. The talking trams cover a route of several kilometres between the Central Deborah goldmine and the Chinese joss house, passing through the heart of Bendigo. The trams are among the oldest still operating in Australia.

WALLS

The oldest known "ha-ha" wall in Australia – a wall running along the bottom of a trench designed to keep animals out of a garden without spoiling the view – is at Werribee Park, 32km west of Melbourne.

If you think the Great Wall of China exists only in China, you've obviously never been to the Kimberley region of Western Australia. About 6km north of Halls Creek is a highly unusual white stone escarpment known to locals as the China Wall. It is a sub-vertical quartz vein projecting above the surrounding rocks and is thought to be part of the largest single fault of its type known anywhere in the world.

WAR MEMORIAL

Ballarat has Australia's longest war memorial – a 22.5km Avenue of Honour consisting of over 3900 trees, one for each man and woman from the city who served in the first World War. Plaques on some of the trees list the names of soldiers, sailors, and nurses killed during conflict. The trees were planted by girls employed at the factory of E. Lucas and Company.

Pine trees grown from seeds brought back from Lone Pine on the Gallipoli Peninsula, where Australians suffered massive casualties during the First World War, can be seen at the Shrine of Remembrance in Melbourne, in front of the Park Motel in the main street of Wangaratta, Victoria, and in the Botanic Gardens at Albury, New South Wales.

WHISKY

The Fingal Hotel, in Fingal, Tasmania, has over 280 different brands of Scotch whisky, thought to be the biggest selection in Australia.

"Titanic" Weathervane

WEATHERVANE

There's a special reason why the weathervane on top of the band rotunda in the main street of Ballarat has a ship instead of the traditional cock. It depicts the Titanic and was erected in memory of the bandsmen who bravely played on as the ill-fated liner plunged into the Atlantic after striking an iceberg during her maiden voyage in 1912. The bandsmen were among 1500 people who drowned.

Another monument to the bandsmen of the Titanic can be seen in a park at Broken Hill.

WINE

The Jesuit winery adjacent to St Aloysius Church at Sevenhill, near Clare, S.A, produces altar wines which are exported worldwide.

Men at work!

'PENCILS! NOTEPAPER! ... MISS PRINGLE – YOU'VE FORGOT THE TOILET ROLLS !!'

'I SHOULD HAVE THOUGHT IT'S PRETTY OBVIOUS WHAT IT IS – IT'S A HEDGEHOG EXTERMINATOR'

For when the saints meet the sinners...

PONTIUS PILATE HAS been canonised as a Saint in the Ethiopian Church – but exactly why remains obscure. Veronica Giullani, however, was beatified by Pope Pius II for good deeds, particularly after she regularly paid tribute to the Lamb of God by taking a real lamb to bed with her, kissing it and suckling it on her breasts!

Bubble bath?

Perhaps the most welcome miracle performed by a Catholic Saint was when St Brigid of Ireland changed her bath water into beer for thirsty visitors to her Kildare abbey in the 1500s.

A virgin for Christmas

Who is the patron saint of virgins? St Nicholas, the original Santa. For some strange reason, he is also the guardian of thieves.

Suffer, you sinner!

Wracked by sexual hallucinations in the thirteenth century, Christine of St. Troud placed herself in a hot oven, strapped herself on a wheel, had herself racked and then hung on the gallows beside a corpse! Still not satisfied, she had herself partly buried in a grave

"I DON'T CARE WHO YOU ARE – YOU'LL HAVE TO QUEUE LIKE THE REST OF US !!

with only her head protruding. Psychoanalysts have since shown that flagellation is often a substitute for sexual intercourse. Confessors even today sometimes force their female parishioners to beat them – as penance for the females!

Saintly Nessie

The Loch Ness monster is no modern invention, as many sceptics would have us believe. Nessie was first reported in AD 565 by none less than St Columba. And if you can't take a saint's word ...

Watch the birdie!

In ancient times, it was believed a person's place in the world beyond could be known by those he left behind if they watched his mouth at the moment he died to see in what form the soul left the body. A red mouse emerging through the mouth indicated a pure soul; a black mouse a polluted soul. A dove appeared only if the person had a saintly soul.

So you think you know a word or two?

WE ALL KNOW about a pride of lions, a swarm of bees and a herd of cattle. But if you really want to impress your friends with your (useless) knowledge of the English language, why not throw in a casual reference to a murder of crows, a sleuth of bears, a skulk of foxes, a building of rooks, a down of hares, a kindle of kittens, an exaltation of larks, or a muster of peacocks. And if someone comes up with a gaggle of geese, don't be fazed – you can easily trump that by pointing out the term refers only to the birds while on the ground. In flight, they become a skein. Before you crow too much, though, test yourself with the following (answers are on Page 192):

What phobia?

Most people know that *claustrophobia* means fear of enclosed spaces and *phobophobia* means fear of fear!. But what about:

1. *Noctiphobia*
2. *Categelophobia*
3. *Opthalmophobia*
4. *Triskaidekaphobia*
5. *Ergophobia*
6. *Ailurophobia*

Animal cries

Horses neigh or whinny, but what sounds are made by:

1. *Deer*
2. *Hares*
3. *Nightingales*
4. *Grouse*
5. *Apes*
6. *Rooks.*

Are you being facetious?

All words in English contain at least one of the vowels "a", "e", "i", "o" and "u". But how many words are there that feature all five in that exact order? Linguists know of only two – do you?

Spelling test

You can spell every numeral from 1 to 100 without using which letter?

Sweat on this one!

Human beings produce between 1.1 and 1.7 litres of sweat a day, through pores on their skin. But other animals sweat through different parts of their bodies – how is this done by:

1. *Dogs*
2. *Cows*
3. *Potaroos (small kangaroos).*

Talking turkey

In Turkey, turkeys are known as "A_______ birds" after the continent from which they were introduced to Europe.

Your reward!

This is to certify that

YOUR NAME TO BE PRINTED HERE

has been awarded the title of

Bachelor of

Useless Information

after passing with

Distinction

the course in

The Dinkum Aussie

Dunny Companion

NICHOLAS REED

Author, The Dinkum Aussie Dunny Companion

Date

This great certificate, issued in YOUR OWN NAME and ready to hang behind your own dunny door, your home bar or anywhere else, can be yours FREE! Just complete the coupon below and mail it with $2.00 postage stamps to cover mailing costs to:

MaxiBooks, PO Box 529, Kiama, NSW 2533

YES, I have studied THE DINKUM AUSSIE DUNNY COMPANION and am qualified to become a BACHELOR OF USELESS INFORMATION. Please make out my certificate in the name of:

(Please print clearly:) ______________________

Name: ______________________

Street ______________________

Town: ______________ P/Code: ______________

Men at work!

"... AND DON'T FORGET – HE'S GOT A BIG RIGHT HAND"

"... AND TO MORROW, CHEF WILL TEACH YOU HOW TO COOK THE BOOKS.."

"I HAVE THIS FEELING THAT EVERYONE IS ONLY INTERESTED IN MY MONEY ....!!"

Why do we say such weird things as ...

EVERYDAY ENGLISH literally translated is often quite incomprehensible to foreigners – and, should you stop to think about exactly what you are saying, sometimes even to native speakers. Here are more of the amazing origins of some of our most common idioms: expressions which say something quite different from their literal meaning.

Haul over the coals: Today, thankfully, the expression means only a reprimand, but its origin goes back to the Middle Ages when heretics were burned at the stake and persons of high rank accused of witchcraft were subjected to the so-called "ordeal by fire" to prove their guilt or innocence. This involved walking barefoot and blindfolded over red-hot plough-shares. Only if the accused person showed no wounds after three days was he or she adjudged innocent. In Sir Walter Scott's *Ivanhoe* there is a reference to a Jew being threatened with a roasting over hot coals; this apparently was a common form of medieval torture to persuade wealthy Jews to provide money needed by kings and barons.

High jinks: Now synonymous with unrestrained merrymaking, high jinks was once a popular game. In his novel *Guy Mannering* (1815), Sir Walter Scott refers to "the ancient and now forgotten pastime of high jinks ... (which) was played in several different ways. Most frequently the dice is thrown by the company, and those

"I TAKE IT YOU'VE HAD ANOTHER DISAGREEMENT WITH THE HAIR-DRESSER, DEAR!!

upon whom the lot fell were obliged to assume and maintain for a time, a certain fictitious character, or to repeat a certain number of fescennine verses in a particular order. If they departed from the characters assigned ... they incurred forfeits"

Hobson's choice: Back in the 16th Century, Thomas Hobson kept a stable in Cambridge. Customers wanting to hire a horse were given Hobson's choice: they had to take the one nearest the door – or go without a mount.

Hoist with his own petard: Meaning to be caught in a trap of your own making, the phrase comes from *Hamlet*: For "tis the sport to have the engineer/Hoist with his own petard; and't shall go hard/But I will delve one yard below their mines/And blow them at the moon" A "petard" was a machine used to blow a hole in an enemy fort; the explosion would "hoist" anyone nearby into the air.

Horns of a dilemma: In Greek, a "lemma" is a proposition so logical it is taken for granted. But when having to choose between two equally undesirable propositions, you are in double (or "di") difficulties. Medieval philosophers likened the problem of such a choice to the horns of a bull – no matter which one you tried to hold down, it would toss and defeat you with the other.

In limbo: Today meaning a kind of no-man's-land, the idiom comes from the early Catholic philosophers' and Dante's depiction of the borders (or limbo) of hell to which were confined the departed spirits of children or those who died before the coming of Christ. They were thus neither in hell nor in heaven.

In the offing: Originally said of ships just visible off the land, the phrase is now used to indicate that something is about to happen.

Kill the goose that lays the golden egg: Aesop's fable tells of the greedy farmer who was not satisfied with getting one golden egg at a time from his amazing goose. Hoping to get all the golden eggs at once, he killed the goose – only to find no eggs inside it.

Kith and kin: Friends and family, from the Old English words "cyth" (acquaintance) and "cynn" (beget, produce).

Know/learn the ropes: This idiom originated in the days of sailing ships when seamen had to know every rope in the rigging. It is still, of course, valid today for yachtsmen.

Last of the Mohicans: Now usually meaning the last of anything, the phrase originally referred to an American Red Indian tribe in the novel *Last of the Mohicans* by James Fenimore Cooper.

Leave no stone unturned: Again the product of Greek mythology (this time as recorded by Euripides), the phrase was used by the Delphic Oracle when consulted by Polycrates after he vanquished Mardonius at Plataea in 477 B.C. but failed to find his treasure. The Oracle advised Polycrates to "leave no stone unturned"; he took the advice literally and so found the hidden loot.

Lick into shape: Now used in the sense of making someone (particularly a child) presentable, it was once widely believed that mother bears literally licked their cubs into the shape of bears. This explanation for the licking action (now known to be a cleaning motion) was recorded, among others, by Avicenna (980-1037, a famous Arab physician and philosopher, in his influential encyclopaedia. The theory was still current at the time of Shakespeare.

Lily-livered: The ancients believed that the liver was not only the seat of love, but that the amount of blood it contained was in direct proportion to the bravery of its owner. A coward's liver would be white and bloodless, like the flower of a lily. As Sir Toby Belch says of timid Sir Andrew Aguecheek in Shakespeare's *Twelfth Night*: "... if he were open'd and you find so much blood in his liver as will clog the foot of a flea, I'll eat the rest of th' anatomy."

Lion's share: One of Aesop's Fables tells of a greedy lion who, after hunting with other animals, demanded all of the prey: one quarter as his prerogative, another quarter for his courage, and a third for his dam and cubs. As to the fourth quarter, the lion dared anyone to dispute it with him – but the animals were too afraid and backed off. Today, the phrase means the largest or choicest share of something.

Lock, stock and barrel: These are the parts that make up an old-fashioned firearm, providing a graphic description of "the whole lot".

Lose face: This saying, translated from the Chinese "tiu lien" and

"DON'T BE SILLY DARLING, OF COURSE THEY DON'T SLEEP IN MY HAT!"

referring to the loss of one's good reputation and standing (a matter of great importance in the East), came into the English language last century. Its companion idiom is to **save face**.

Mad as a hatter: To make felt hats, hatters in days gone by used mercury, which afflicts the nervous system, giving the appearance of madness. The phrase was made popular by Lewis Caroll in *Alice's Adventures in Wonderland* (1865), but it was used in much earlier writings.

Mad as a March hare: Another idiom popularised in *Alice's Adventures in Wonderland*, this apparently originated because of the courtship antics of English hares during March, their main breeding season. The phrase goes back to Chaucer.

Made a scapegoat: Used to describe someone who is blamed for the misdeeds of others, the expression has its origins in the Old Testament. During a religious ceremony the sins of the Israelites were transferred to a goat, which was then set free and "let go for a scapegoat into the wilderness".

Naked truth: An old fable recorded by Horace tells how, when Truth and Falsehood went swimming, Falsehood emerged first and walked off wearing Truth's clothes. Rather than don Falsehood's garments, Truth went naked.

"YOU'LL SIMPLY LOVE THE GIBSON'S – THEY'RE TERRIBLY UNCONVENTIONAL..."

Mind your P's and Q's: There are several theories about the origin of this idiom, first recorded in 1789. The generally accepted one refers to the practise of compositors to read upside down the type they are setting, which could easily create confusion between the letters "p" and "q". Hence the warning to printers' apprentices. Another explanation says publicans adding up their accounts had to make sure they distinguished between "pints" and "quarts" of beer; so too, if they were wise, did the customers!

Mud in your eye! This popular toast originated in the trenches during the First World War as an ironic comment by the troops about the muddy conditions on the Western front.

Nail your colours to the mast: Now meaning to support openly a particular course of action or organisation, the phrase comes from sailing ship days when crews would literally nail the flag to the mast to prevent it being lowered as a sign of surrender.

Neither rhyme nor reason: Not impressed by a book, Sir Thomas More (chancellor of King Henry VIII) suggested the author turn it into rhyme. He did so, prompting Sir Thomas to remark: "...now it is rhyme; before it was neither rhyme nor reason."

Not enough room to swing a cat: Until 1875, a whip known as the cat-'o-nine-tails (usually abbreviated to "cat") was used to punish sailors on board Royal Navy ships, which were not noted for an abundance of space. Novelist Tobias Smollett (1721-71), who spent considerable time at sea, was one of the first to use the phrase to describe a confined space.

Not one jot or tittle: This Biblical idiom – meaning not even the tiniest amount – is found in the Gospel of St Matthew where Christ says: "Till heaven and earth pass, one jot or one tittle shall in no wise pass from the law, till all be fulfilled." Jot stands for "iota", the smallest letter in the Greek alphabet, and tittle (from the Latin "titilus") for the dot above it.

CODED VERSES

These few lines from Banjo Paterson poems are in code. One letter of the alphabet is substituted for the correct letter. One way to break the code is to look for repeated letters. "E" is most often used. A single lettered word would be "A" or "I" and a repeated three lettered word could be "THE" or "AND"

Poem 1:

(To start you off with this puzzle, "M" is substituted for "A".)

WAPXP FMO LGBPLPDW MW WAP OWMWEGD, JGX WAP
FGXK AMK CMOOPK MXGZDK
WAMW WAP QGYW JXGL GYK XPTXPW AMK TGW MFMR.

Poem 2:

(To start you off with this puzzle, "G" is substituted for "I")

G'H NGEO MS JOO BLOOQ BLWJJ WBWGQ
WQH ZWMAV ANOWL ZWMOL LTQ
WZWR KLSF MVGJ TQVSNR DNWGQ
WQH KNGOJ, WQH HTJM, WQH JTQ.

Answers on Page 191

The dangerous art of pillow talk

Is it not strange that desire should so many years outlive performance?

-SHAKESPEARE.

Sex is hard for one. But it's good for two.

T-SHIRT INSCRIPTION.

If a woman hasn't got a tiny streak of a harlot in her, she's a dry stick as a rule.

D.H. LAWRENCE.

There's a sexual revolution going on, and I think that with out current foreign policy, we'll probably be sending troops in there any minute to break it up.

- MEL BROOKS.

Sex is one of the nine reasons for reincarnation, the other eight are unimportant.

- AUTHOR HENRY MILLER.

The orgasm has replaced the cross as the organ of longing and the image of fulfilment.

- MALCOLM MUGGERIDGE.

Sex – the poor man's polo.

- CLIFFORD ODETTS.

"LET'S HOPE YOUR CAR PERFORMS BETTER THAN YOU DO!!"

There are a number of mechanical devices which increase sexual arousal, particularly in women. Chief among these is the Merccedes Benz 380 SL Convertible.

- P.J. O'ROURKE.

All this humorless document really proves is: (a) that all men lie when they are asked about their adventures in amour, and (b) that pedagogues are singly naive and credulous creatures.

- H.L. MENCKEN ON THE KINSEY REPORT.

Sexuality is the lyricism of the masses.

- CHARLES BAUDELAIRE.

What most men desire is a virgin who is a whore.

- EDWARD DAHLBERG.

People who throw kisses are hopelessly lazy.

BOB HOPE.

I could be content if we might procreate like trees, without conjunction, or that there were many ways to perpetuate the world without this trivial and vulgar way of coition.

· SIR THOMAS BROWN (1672).

It has to be admitted that we English have sex on the brain, which is a very unsatisfactory place to have it.

· MALCOLM MUGGERIDGE.

Continental people have sex life: the English have hot water bottles.

· GEORGE MIKES.

What comes first in a relationship is lust, then more lust.

· JACQUILINE BISSET.

A man marries to have a home, but also because he doesn't want to be bothered with sex and all that sort of thing.

· W. SOMERSET MAUGHAM.

I'd rather have a cup of tea and a good conversation.

· BOY GEORGE.

If you cannot find love with a man or a woman then find it in house plants. It won't be the same thing but when you go to bed at night you may be less disappointed.

TINA TURNER.

When it's a choice between food and sex, food will win all the time.

· SHELLEY WINTERS.

CORRECT ME IF I'M WRONG – BUT, SIR, DID ASK FOR ANYTHING IN A SKIRT, DID HE NOT ?"

I make time for sex between pictures or when I'm bored.

· CHARLIE CHAPLIN.

There is no greater not keener pleasure than that of bodily love – and none which is more irrational.

· PLATO.

'Tis the devil inspires this evanescent ardor, in order to divert the parties from prayer.

· MARTIN LUTHER.

Sex is like a candy box. When it's open, why resist?

· MICK JAGGER.

I thought of losing my virginity as a career move.

- MADONNA.

I like the boys and the boys like me. Men are exciting, and the gal who denies that men are exciting is either a lady with no corpuscles or a statue.

- LANA TURNER.

Bed is for sleeping on.

- ELVIS PRESLEY.

Is that all there is to it?

- PRINCE CHARLES to a confidante.

Sex? It's best in the afternoon coming out of the shower.

- RONALD REAGAN.

I'd rather win an Oscar than a pretty girl. One is permanent, the other is not.

- JACK NICHOLSON.

This sort of thing might be tolerated by the French, but we are British, thank God!

- VISCOUNT MONTGOMERY on homosexuality.

If sex is all wrong and dirty, then I suppose we will have to rethink the human race.

- KENNETH TYNAN.

I'm tired, send one of them home.

- MAE WEST, on hearing ten men were waiting for her at home.

What do you give the man who's had everyone?

- Rod Stewart's ex-wife, ALANA.

"WHAT A PLACE TO WORK ... NO HOT DRINKS VENDING MACHINE ... NO LUNCHEON VOUCHERS ... NO SEXUAL HARASSMENT ... !"

All this fuss about sleeping together. For physical pleasure, I'd rather go to my dentist any day.

· EVELYN WAUGH, in "Vile Bodies"

Sexual intercourse is like bicycle racing: the more you do it, the better you get.

· ERNEST HEMINGWAY.

The more sex becomes a non-issue in people's lives, the happier they are.

· Shirley MacLaine.

Sex? I think it's here to stay.

· GROUCHO MARX.

DOUBLE MEANINGS

HOW TO PLAY

Find a word which answers both clues:

1. Base of a ladder; imperial measure
2. Angry; religious symbol
3. Movement of the sea; greeting
4. Imperial measure; animal enclosure
5. Outfall of river; part of the head
6. Season; flow of water
7. Recline; furniture item

1 ______________
2. ______________
3. ______________
4. ______________
5. ______________
6. ______________
7 ______________

Answers on Page 192

ON THE TUCKER TRACK

An hilarious outback tale by HENRY LAWSON

STEELMAN AND SMITH, professional wanderers from New Zealand, took a run over to Australia one year to have a look at the country, and drifted Out Back, and played cards and headin' 'em at the shearing sheds (while pretending to be strangers to each other), and sold eye-water and unpatented medicine, and worked the tucker tracks. They had a streak of bad luck at West-o'-Sunday Station, where they were advised (by the boss and about fifty excited shearers) to go east, and not to stop till they reached the coast. They were tramping along the track towards Bourke; they were very hard-up and had had to battle for tucker and tobacco along the track. They came to a lonely shanty, about two camps west of Bourke.

"We'll turn off into the scrub and strike the track the other side of the shanty and come back to it," said Steelman. "You see, if they see us coming into Bourke they'll say to themselves, 'Oh, we're never likely to see these chaps again,' and they won't give us anything, or, perhaps, only a pinch of tea or sugar in a big lump of paper. There's some women that can never see a tucker-bag, even if you hold it right under their noses. But if they see us going Out Back they'll reckon that we'll get a shed likely as not, and we'll be sure to call there with our cheques coming back. I hope the old man's got the lumbago, or sciatica, or something."

"Why?" asked Smith. "Because whenever I see an old man poking around the place on a stick I always make for him straight and inquire about his trouble; and no matter what complaint he's got, my old man suffered from it for years. It's pretty hard graft listening to an old man with a pet leg, but I find it pays; and I always finish up by advising him to try St. Jacob's oil. Perhaps he's been trying it for years, but that doesn't matter; the consultation works out all right all the same, and there's never been a remedy tried yet but I've got another.

"I've got a lot of Maori and blackfellow remedies in my mind, and when they fail I can fall back on the Chinese; and, if that isn't enough, I've got a list of my grandmother's remedies that she wrote down for me when I was leaving home, and I kept it for a curiosity. It took her three days to write them, and I reckon they'll fill the bill.

"You don't want a shave. You look better with that stubble on. You needn't say anything; just stand by and wear your usual expression, and if they ask me what's the matter with my mate I'll fix up a disease for you to have, and get something extra on your account, poor beggar!

"I wish we had a chap with us that could sing a bit and run the gamut on a fiddle or something. With a sicklylooking fish like you to stand by and look interesting and die slowly of consumption all the time, and me do the talking, we'd be able to travel from one end of the Bush to the other, and live on the fat of the land. I wouldn't cure you for a hundred pounds."

They reached the shanty, and there, sure enough, was an old man pottering round with a list to starboard. He was working with a hoe inside a low paling fence round a sort of garden. Steelman and Smith stopped outside the fence.

"Good day, boss!"

"'Day."

"It's hot."

"It's hot."

So far it was satisfactory. He was a little man, with a wiry, red beard. He might have been a Scandinavian.

"You seem to be a bit lame," said Steelman. "Hurt your foot?"

"Naw," said the old man. "It's an old thing."

"Ah!" said Steelman, "lumbago, I suppose? My father suffered cruel from it for years."

"Naw," said the old man, moving closer to the fence. "It ain't in me back; the trouble's with me leg."

"Oh!" said Steelman. "One a bit shorter than the other?"

"Well, yes. It seems to be wearin' a bit shorter. I must see to it."

"Hip disease, perhaps?" said Steelman. "A brother o'mine had –"

"Naw, it's not in the hip," said the old man. "My leg's gone at the knee."

"Oh! stiff joint; I know what that is. Had a touch of it once myself. An uncle of mine was nearly crippled with it. He used to use St. Jacob's Oil. Ever try St. Jacob's Oil?"

"Naw," said the old man, "not that I know of. I've used linseed oil though."

"Linseed oil!" said Steelman; "I never heard of that for stiff knee. How do you use it?"

"Use it raw," said the old man. "Raw linseed oil; I've rubbed it in, and I've soaked me leg in it."

"Soaked your leg in it!" said Steelman. "And did it do any good?"

"Well, it seems to preserve it – keeps it from warping, and it wears better – and it makes it heavier. It seemed a bit too light before."

Steelman nudged Smith under cover of the palings. The old man was evidently a bit ratty.

"Well, I hope your leg will soon be all right, boss," said Steelman.

"Thank you," said the old man, "but I don' think there's much hope. I suppose you want some tucker?"

"Well, yes," said Steelman, rather taken aback by the old man's sudden way of putting it. "We're hard up."

"Well, come along to the house and I'll see if I can get yer something," said the old man; and they walked along outside the fence and he bobbed along inside, till he came to a little gate at the comer. He opened the gate and stumped out. He had a wooden leg. He wore his trouser leg down over it, and the palings had hidden the bottom from Steelman and Smith.

He wanted them to stay to dinner, but Steelman didn't feel comfortable, and thanked him, and said they'd rather be getting on (Steelman always spoke for Smith); so the old man gave them some cooked meat, bread, and a supply of tea and sugar. Steelman watched his face very close, but he never moved a muscle. But when they looked back he was leaning on his hoe, and seemed to be shaking.

"Took you back a bit, Steely, didn't it?" suggested Smith.

"How do you make that out?" snorted Steelman, turning on him suddenly. "I knew a carpenter who used to soak his planes in raw linseed oil to preserve them and give them weight. There's nothing funny about that."

Smith rubbed his head.

STEP LADDER

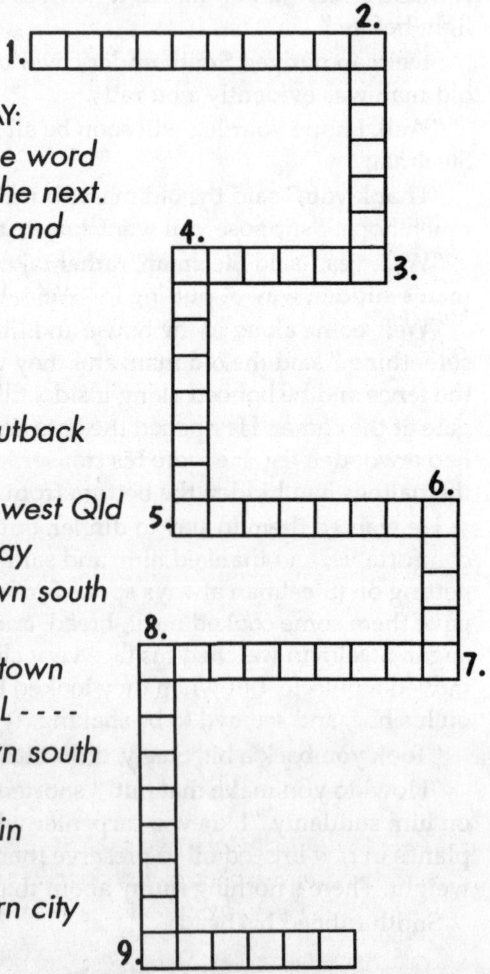

HOW TO PLAY:

The last letter of one word is the first letter of the next. Answers are towns and cities of Australia.

Clues:

1. *Queensland's outback races*
2. *Jewel in central west Qld*
3. *Northern gateway*
4. *NSW wheat town south of Moree*
5. *NSW sapphire town*
6. *Vic surfing spot L - - - -*
7. *WA coastal town south of Norseman*
8. *SA satellite city in Adelaide*
9. *Tas. south eastern city*

Answers on Page 192

War and Peace

FRANCE lost the battle of Waterloo not because of Wellington's brilliant campaigning, but because Napoleon suffered from haemorrhoids. Medical historian Rudolph Marx says on the day of the battle Napoleon suffered from a severe attack of haemorrhoids, which meant he could not mount a horse to exploit a weakness in the British flank.

For valour

Until 1942 Victoria Cross medals (instituted in 1856) were made from the metal of guns captured at Sebastopol in 1855 during the Crimean War.

Captain (later Sir) Neville Howse, serving with the New South Wales Lancers, won Australia's first Victoria Cross at Vredefort, South Africa, on 24 July 1900 during the Boer War.

Accounting for victory

Getting ahead in the army of ancient Scythia meant collecting as many heads as possible on the battlefield, because loot was divided among soldiers on the basis of their enemy head count.

Red Indians scalped their victims to show how many they had killed. Ethiopian warriors, on the other hand, cut off the penises from their

YOU MEAN TO SAY YOU EXCHANGED ME FOR A JAMES LAST LP. ?!!

victims and strung them along the ends of their spears.

What a price to pay

More money was spent on materials during the Second World War than in all of mankind's wars before that put together. The total cost has been calculated at $1.5 million million.

Firewater!

The phrase "Dutch courage", which means be daring after having a few drinks, refers to a former Dutch military custom of drinking spirits before going into battle.

Australia's first ...

War vessel, the *Spitfire*, a 60-ton armed ketch built for the New South Wales colonial government, was launched in Sydney on 4 April 1855. Thirteen months later the armed sloop *Victoria*, Victoria's first warship, arrived at Port Phillip from Britain.

Wedded bliss?

HAVING a woman ask a man to marry her during a leap year was not enough break with convention for the Scots. In 1288 a law was passed in Scotland stating that if the man refused the maiden's offer without good cause, he had to pay her the sum of one pound. Some ugly women must have made a fortune!

Naked truth

Tuareg women are famed for their independence. When a husband insults his wife in public, she will usually strip off all her clothes and walk around stark naked until he apologises – with an acceptable gift.

A kiss is just a ...

In Puritan New England in the 17th century, a man was placed in the stocks for two hours – because he kissed his wife in public.

Bands of matrimony

Adultery can be a pain in the neck for women if they're a member of Africa's Tupuri tribe. The punishment for cheating on her husband? The erring wife has a brass ring fitted around her neck

– which she has to wear for the rest of her life.

Peter the Great of Russia had a gruesome way to remind his wife of the penalty for adultery. He had the head of her lover cut off, then pickled in a bottle of alcohol and placed at her bedside.

My wife, my mother-in-law and I

England's King Ethelred the Unready spent his wedding night in bed with his wife – and her mother.

Wife strife

English writer Samuel Pepys in the 1600s often complained in his famous diary that his wife was giving him strife– because he loved squeezing their maid's breasts in the morning.

What a stud!

Is this a potency record? Russian peasant Feodor Vassilyev's fathered 69 children by the same wife whose name, in the true sexist style of the 18th century, was not recorded. She had four quadruplets, seven triplets, sixteen pairs of twins – and almost all survived to adulthood.

Innocent Mrs Caesar

Caesar's wife must be above suspicion: When rumours linked Pompeia, second wife of Julius Caesar, with a scandal involving Publius Clodius in 62 B.C., the then Roman praetor divorced her. According to the historians Suetonius and Plutarch, Caesar acted not because he thought his wife guilty of infidelity, but because he could not bear anyone even suspecting her.

'MELANIE ! DON'T INTERRUPT DADDY WHEN HE'S TRYING TO DO AWAY WITH HIMSELF ... !

Stop nagging, or else...

About 300 years ago the Sultan of Turkey, sick of nagging wives, had his entire harem drowned. Not that he became celibate after that – he soon created an even bigger (and much more obedient) harem.

Just call Mumbo Jumbo

Mumbo Jumbo today means a lot of nonsense, but to African tribes it was a very realistic and frightening spectacle that helped to keep women's lib at bay. According to the famous explorer Mungo Park, Mumbo Jumbo was called in by a husband when a woman in his household became too quarrelsome or disobedient. Actually, he was a friend or relative of the husband, who disguised himself and arrived at nightfall making horrible noises. At his orders, all the women were assembled, and then the offender was "stripped naked, tied to a post, and severely scourged with Mumbo's rod, amidst the shouts and derision of the whole family"

CODED VERSES

These few lines from a famous Australian poem are in code. One letter of the alphabet is substituted for the correct letter. One way to break the code is to look for repeated letters. "E" is most often used. A single lettered word would be "A" or "I" and a repeated three lettered word could be "THE" or "AND"

(To start you off with this puzzle, "L" is substituted for "E".)

EL TOP PELOKDHF TELH D XHLT EDW, PR D
PLHS SEL YLSSLK SR EDW

MCPS RH PJLN, OVVKLPPLV OP BRYYRTP,
"NYOHNZ, RB SEL RQLKBYRT"

Answers on Page 192

'WITH CHARLES AND I IT WAS LOVE AT FIRST SIGHT OF HIS BANK ACCOUNT'.

What Dagwood did for love

Dagwood Bumstead (of comic book fame) was not always poor, overworked, browbeaten and given to scoffing giant sandwiches. His first public appearance way back in 1930 was as a carefree playboy and prospective heir to millions. Then along came a pretty but poor flapper named Blondie – and Dagwood was hooked. His disapproving parents gave him a choice: love or money. Love (of course) triumphed, Dagwood married Blondie, was disinherited – and as a true battler has become part of the everyday lives of millions of people all over the world.

Naughty Poms

In the eighth century, Pope Boniface complained that the English "utterly despise matrimony ... and utterly refuse to have legitimate wives, and continue to live in lechery and adultery after the manner of neighing horses and braying asses ..."

Big Bill and the Golden Horseshoes

BIG BILL JOHNSON was the most flamboyant gold digger ever to work an Australian claim. When he struck it rich, he proved it to the world in a way that made misers of those who celebrated their wealth by lighting cigars with ten pound notes.

The year was 1855 and Victoria was delirious with gold fever. Ports were choked with ships abandoned by their crews, who joined their passengers and thousands of Australians in a mad rush to the interior where fortune awaited a lucky few.

One of them was Big Bill Johnson, a kind-hearted giant who pegged a bonanza of a claim in the bed of Woolshed Creek, near the town of Beechworth. So rich was the yield that Big Bill within days bought up most of the town's supply of buckets – because he needed containers in which to store his gold!

Soon he was employing 50 men, paying out more than £500 a week in wages. Big Bill became the richest man on the Ovens Valley field, worth more than £70,000 – many times a millionaire by today's standards.

The lucky digger regularly shouted his mates a dozen or so bottles of champagne at one of Beechworth's many pubs. But he really turned on a bash on the day a local shopkeeper named Cameron was elected the area's first Member of the Victorian Parliament.

Big Bill called in a blacksmith and pointed to a pile of gleaming gold. "I want four horseshoes," he said. "Solid gold ones."

When the shoes were ready, they weighed some 32 ounces – worth more than $15,000 today. Big Bill ordered them fitted to a piebald horse, which he then offered to the new MP for his triumphant ride from the diggings to Beechworth.

Hundreds of diggers lined the route to cheer the horse and rider, then followed them all the way into town. There Big Bill turned on a shout that consumed 300 bottles of champagne at £1 a bottle. The barman simply knocked the heads of the bottles and emptied them into buckets – enabling the thirsty diggers to dip in and fill up their beer mugs!

When the horseshoes were later removed, it was found that three ounces of gold had worn away during the journey. But that did not bother Big Bill – he simply smiled and said: "There's plenty more where that came from."

But, in the end, Big Bill put his entire fortune back into the ground. He left the Woolshed diggings with his fortune, joining rushes to one new field after the other. But his luck never returned and when he died in Queensland years later, he was almost penniless.

What finally became of the golden horseshoes no one knows. Plaster copies remain in Beechworth's Burke Museum, while on the road to the Woolshed diggings a monument featuring a giant gilded horseshoe commemorates the amazing journey that has become part of Australian folklore.

HOW TO PLAY:

The last letter of one word is the first letter of the next. Answers are towns and cities of Australia.

STEP LADDER

Clues:

1. Nth Qld sugar cane town
2. The - - - - - (Australian bush) slang
3. Large sea bird
4. - - - - - - - Desert
5. Aust marsupial
6. Snowy mountains town
7. North Qld city
8. Sir - - - - - - Hillary
9. - - - - - - - Downs (area in south east Qld)

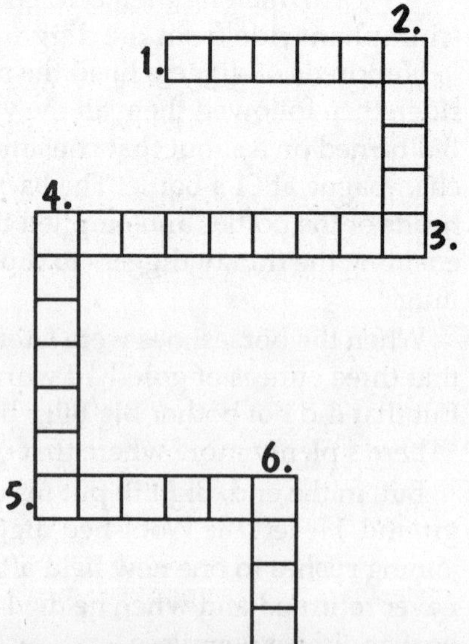

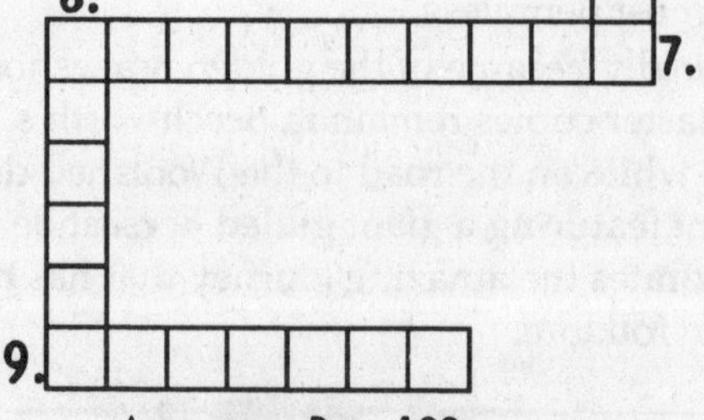

Answers on Page 192

Royal flush!

FOURTEEN certainly meant something to King Louis XIV of France. Not only was he the 14th king of that name, but he ascended the throne in 1643, which adds up to 14, as does the date of his death in 1715, and the length of his 77 year reign. He was born in 1638 and died in 1715, which added together totals 3353 – the sum of which again equals 14!

Potty portrait

Hearing the Duchess de Polignac lavishly praising the American statesman Benjamin Franklin, a jealous King Louis VI of France presented her with a portrait of Franklin – painted inside the bowl of a chamber pot!

Well done, good and faithful servant

Russian Czar Ivan the Terrible was so proud of St Basil's Cathedral in Moscow, which he had built in the 16th Century, that he had the architect's eyes put out to prevent him ever creating a similar or better church. Some reward, indeed!

Fatherly pride

Carlo Buonaparte, an impoverished Corsican lawyer, was perhaps the most successful father in history, if titles are anything to go by. He fathered an emperor, three kings, a queen, and two duchesses. The emperor, of course, was Napoleon, who gave all his brothers and sisters titles and top positions in his far-flung empire.

Great ... or plain Simple?

The title Charlemagne or Charles the Great is the accolade bestowed by history on the Frankish king who reigned as Holy Roman Emperor in the 8th Century. But after him the royal splendour rapidly declined, at least judging by the popular names for his successors: Charles the Bald, Louis the Stammerer, Charles the Fat, and Charles the Simple.

I spy with my little eye...

Talk about a right royal peeping Tom. Catherine de Medici drilled a hole in her bedroom floor to observe her husband making love to his mistress in the room below.

Card trick

Ever wondered why the people pictured in a modern pack of cards look kind of old fashioned? The figures are dressed in fashions popular during the 15th century reign of Henry VII, whose wife Elizabeth of York is represented by the Queen in the pack.

We were amused

Which famous married couple last century delighted in this riddle: "Who's the greediest glutton for love in bed?" answered by: "Look in the mirror, your face is red!" The couple? Queen Victoria and her consort, Prince Albert.

Quote Unquote

My only contribution to British life has been to improve the rear lights on lorries.

· Prince Philip.

My name is Andrew Edward, my father is a gentleman farmer and my mother does not work!

- A jesting Prince Andrew in France.

I can pray when I'm fishing, but I can't fish in church.

- Prince Charles.

My children are not royal, they just happen to have the Queen for an aunt.

· Princess Margaret.

I have tiny boobs and big shoulders.

· Princess Michael of Kent.

She's more royal than the rest of us.

- The Queen of Princess Michael of Kent.

I suppose I'll now be known as Charley's aunt?

- Princess Margaret on hearing what the Queen's first child would be called

It looks rather damp.

- The Queen on seeing the Niagara Falls.

I've learnt the way a monkey learns – by watching its parents.

· Prince Charles.

Most disappointing.

- The Queen's reaction to the Sphinx in Egypt.

The biggest waste of water in the country by far. You spend half a pint and flush two gallons.

- Prince Philip about dunnies.

I don't believe in fashion, full stop.

- Prince Charles.

If you stay here much longer you'll go back with slitty eyes.

- Prince Philip to British students during a visit to China.

I don't know what you two old queens are doing down there, but this old Queen is dying of thirst.

- The Queen Mother to her footmen while waiting for her nightcap.

I have as much privacy as a goldfish in a bowl.

- Princess Margaret.

Basically, I am a carpenter.

- Lord Snowdon.

I may be a lot of things, but I'm not boring.

- Princess Michael of Kent.

Never refuse an invitation to sit down, and take every opportunity to relieve yourself.

- Queen Mary to the Duke of Windsor.

A woman can never be too rich or too thin.

- The Duchess of Windsor.

That Pretty GIRL In The Army

By Henry Lawson

Now I often sit at Watty's, when the night is very near,
With a head that's full of jingles – and the fumes of bottled beer;
For I always have a fancy that, If I am over there
When the Army prays for Watty, I'm included in the prayer.
It would take a lot of praying, lots of thumping on the drum,
To prepare our sinful, straying, erring souls for Kingdom Come.
But I love my fellow-sinners! and I hope, upon the whole,
That the Army gets a hearing when it prays for Watty's soul

WHEN THE WORLD WAS WIDE.

THE SALVATION ARMY does good business in some of the out-back towns of the great pastoral wastes of Australia. There's the thoughtless, careless generosity of the bushman, whose pockets don't go far enough down his trousers (that's what's the matter with him), and who contributes to anything that comes along, without troubling to ask questions, like long Bob Brothers of Bourke, who, chancing to be "a Protestant by rights," unwittingly subscribed towards the erection of a new Catholic church, and being chaffed for his mistake, said:

"Ah, well, I don't suppose it'll matter a hang in the end, anyway it goes. I ain't got nothink agenst the Roming Carflicks."

There's the shearer, fresh with his cheque from a cut-out shed, gloriously drunk and happy, in love with all the world, and ready to subscribe towards any creed and shout for all bands – including Old Nick if he happened to come along. There's the shearer, half-drunk and inclined to be nasty, who has got the wrong end of all things with a tight grip, and who flings a shilling in the face of out-back conventionality (as he thinks) by chucking a bob into the Salvation Army ring. Then he glares round to see if be can catch anybody winking behind his back. There's the cynical joker, a queer mixture, who contributes generously and tempts the reformed boozer afterwards. There's the severe-faced old station-hand – in clean shirt and neckerchief and white moleskins – in for his annual or semi-annual spree, who contributes on principle, and then drinks religiously until his cheque is gone and the horrors are come. There's the shearer, feeling mighty bad after a spree, and in danger of seeing things when he tries to go to sleep. He has dropped ten or twenty pounds over bar counters and at cards, and he now "chucks" a repentant shilling into the ring, with a very private and rather vague sort of feeling that something might come of it. There's the stout, contented, good-natured publican, who tips the Army as if it were a barrel-organ. And there are others and other reasons – black sheep and ne'er-do-wells – and faint echoes of other times in Salvation Army tunes.

Bourke, the metropolis of the Great Scrubs, on the banks of the Darling River, about five hundred miles from Sydney, was suffering from a long drought when I was there in ninety-two; and the heat may or may not have been another cause contributing to the success, from a business point of view, of the Bourke garrison. There was much beer boozing – and, besides, it was vaguely understood (as most things are vaguely understood out there in the drought-haze) that the place the Army came to save us from was hotter than Bourke. We didn't hanker to go to a hotter place than Bourke. But that year there was an extraordinary reason for the Army's great financial success there.

She was a little girl, nineteen or twenty, I should judge, the prettiest girl I ever saw in the Army, and one of the prettiest I've ever seen out of it. She had the features of an angel, but her expression was wonderfully human, sweet and sympathetic. Her big grey eyes were sad with sympathy for sufferers and sinners, and her poke bonnet was full of bunchy, red-gold hair. Her first appearance was somewhat dramatic – perhaps the Army arranged it so.

The Army used to pray, and thump the drum, and sing, and take up collections every evening outside Watty

Bothways's Hotel, the Carriers' Arms. They performed longer and more often outside Watty's than any other pub in town – perhaps because Watty was considered the most hopeless publican and his customers the hardest crowd of boozers in Bourke. The band generally began to play about dusk. Watty would lean back comfortably in a basket easy-chair on his wide veranda, and clasp his hands, in a calm, contented way, while the Army banged the drum and got steam up, and whilst, perhaps, there was a barney going on in the bar, or a bloodthirsty fight in the backyard. On such occasions there was something like an indulgent or fatherly expression on his fat and usually emotionless face. And by and by he'd move his head gently and doze. The banging and the singing seemed to soothe him, and the praying, which was often very personal, never seemed to disturb him in the least.

Well, it was about dusk one day; it had been a terrible day, a hundred and something startling in the shade, but there came a breeze after sunset. There had been several dozen buckets of water thrown on the veranda floor and the ground outside. Watty was seated in his accustomed place when the Army arrived. There was no barney in the bar because there was a fight in the backyard, and that claimed the attention of all the customers.

The Army prayed for Watty and his clients; then a reformed drunkard started to testify against publicans and all their works. Watty settled himself comfortably, folded his hands, and leaned back and dozed.

The fight was over, and the chaps began to drop round to the bar. The man who was saved waved his arms, and danced round and howled.

"Ye-es!" he shouted hoarsely. "The publicans, and boozers, and gamblers, and sinners may think that Bourke is hot, but hell is a thousand times hotter! I tell you —"

"Oh, Lord!" said Mitchell, the shearer, and he threw a penny into the ring.

"Ye-es! I tell you that hell is a million times hotter than Bourke! I tell you —"

"Oh, look here," said a voice from the background, "that won't wash. Why, don't you know that when the Bourke people die they send back for their blankets?"

The saved brother glared round. "I hear a freethinker speaking, my friends," he said. Then, with sudden inspiration and renewed energy, "I hear the voice of a freethinker. Show me the face of a freethinker," he yelled, glaring round Me a hunted, hungry man. "Show me the face of a freethinker, and I'll tell you what he is."

Watty hitched himself into a more comfortable position and clasped his hands on his knee and closed his eyes again.

"Ya-a-a-s!" shrieked the brand. "I tell you, my friends, I can tell a freethinker by his face. Show me the face of a —"

At this point there was an interruption. One-eyed, or Wall-eyed Bogan, who had a broken nose, and the best side of whose face was reckoned the ugliest and most sinister — One-eyed Bogan thrust his face forward from the ring of darkness into the torchlight of salvation. He had got the worst of a drawn battle; his nose and mouth were bleeding, and his good eye was damaged.

"Look at my face!" he snarled, with dangerous earnestness. "Look at my face! That's the face of a freethinker, and I don't care who knows it. Now! what have you got to say against my face, 'Man-without-a-Shirt?'"

The brother drew back. He had been known in the north-west in his sinful days as "Man-without-a-Shirt," alias "Shirty," or "The Dirty Man," and was flabbergasted at being recognized in speech. Also, he had been in a shearing-shed and in a shanty orgy with One-eyed Bogan, and knew the man.

Now most of the chaps respected the Army, and, indeed, anything that looked like religion, but the Bogan's face, as representing free thought, was a bit too sudden for them. There were sounds on the opposite side of the ring as from men being smitten repeatedly and rapidly below the belt, and long Tom Hall and one or two others got away into the darkness in the background, where Tom rolled helplessly on the grass and sobbed.

It struck me that Bogan's face was more the result of free speech than anything else.

The Army was about to pray when the Pretty Girl stepped forward, her eyes shining with indignation and enthusiasm. She had arrived by the evening train, and had been standing shrinkingly behind an Army lass of fifty Australian summers, who was about six feet high, flat and broad, and had a square face, and a mouth like a joint in boiler plates.

The Pretty Girl stamped her pretty foot on the gravel, and her eyes flashed in the torchlight.

"You ought to be ashamed of yourselves," she said. "Great big men like you to be going on the way you are. If you were ignorant or poor, as I've seen people, there might be some excuse for you. Haven't you got any mothers, or sisters, or wives to think of? What sort of a life is this you lead? Drinking, and gambling, and fighting, and swearing your lives away! Do you ever think of God and the time when you were children? Why don't you make homes? Look at that man's face!" (she pointed suddenly at Bogan, who collapsed and sidled behind his mates out of the light). "Look at that man's face! Is it a face for a Christian? And you help and encourage him to fight. You're worse than he is. Oh, it's brutal. It's – it's wicked. Great big men like you, you ought to be ashamed of yourselves."

Long Bob Brothers – about six-foot-four – the longest and most innocent there, shrunk down by the wag and got his inquiring face out of the light. The Pretty Girl fluttered on for a few moments longer, greatly excited, and then stepped back, seemingly much upset, and was taken under the wing of the woman with the boiler-plate mouth.

It was a surprise, and very sudden. Bogan slipped round to the backyard, and was seen bathing his battered features at the pump. The rest wore the expression of men who knew that something unusual has happened, but don't know what, and are waiting vacantly for developments except Tom Hall, who had recovered and returned. He stood looking over the head of the ring of bushmen, and apparently taking the same critical interest in the girl as he would in a fight – his expression was such as a journalist might wear who is getting exciting copy.

The Army had it all their own way for the rest of the evening, and made a good collection. The Pretty Girl stood smiling round with shining eyes as the bobs and tanners dropped in, and then, being shoved forward by the flat woman, she thanked us sweetly, and said we were good fellows, and that she was sorry for some things she'd said to us. Then she retired, fluttering and very much flushed, and hid herself behind the hard woman – who, by the way, had an excrescence on her upper lip which might have stood for a rivet.

Presently the Pretty Girl came from behind the big woman and stood watching things with glistening eyes. Some of the chaps on the opposite side of the ring moved a little to one side and an were careful not to meet her eye – not to be caught looking at her – lest she should be embarrassed. Watty had roused himself a little at the sound of a strange voice in the Army (and such a clear, sweet voice too!) and had a look; then he settled back peacefully again, but it was noticed that he didn't snore that evening.

And, when the Army prayed, the Pretty Girl knelt down with the rest on the gravel. One or two tall bushmen bowed their heads as if they had to, and One-eyed Bogan, with the blood washed from his face, stood with his hat off, glaring round to see if he could catch anyone sniggering.

Mitchell, the shearer, said afterwards that the whole business made him feel for the moment like he felt sometimes in the days when he used to feel things.

The town discussed the Pretty Girl in the Army that night and for many days thereafter, but no one could find out who she was or where she belonged – except that she came from Sydney last. She kept her secret, if she had one, very close – or else the other S.A. women were not to be pumped. She lived in skillion-rooms at the back of the big weather-board Salvation Army barracks with two other "lassies," who did washing and sewing and nursing, and went shabby, and half starved themselves, and were baked in the heat, like scores of women in the bush, and even as hundreds of women, suffering from religious mania, slave and stint in city slums, and neglect their homes, husbands and children – for the glory of Booth.

The Pretty Girl was referred to as Sister Hannah by the Army people, and came somehow to be known by sinners as "Miss Captain." I don't know whether that was her real name or what rank she held in the Army, if indeed she held any.

She sold *War Crys*, and the circulation doubled in a day. One-eyed Bogan, being bailed up unexpectedly, gave her "half a caser" for a Cry, and ran away without the paper or the change. Jack Mitchell bought a Cry for the first time in his life, and read it. He said he found some of the articles intensely realistic, and many of the statements were very interesting. He said he read one or two things in the Cry that he didn't know before. Tom Hall, taken unawares, bought three Crys from the Pretty Girl, and blushed to find it fame.

Little Billy Woods, the Labourers' Union secretary who had a poetic temperament and more than the average bushman's reverence for higher things – Little Billy Woods told me in a burst of confidence that he generally had two feelings, one after the other, after encountering that girl. One was that unfathomable far-away feeling of loneliness and longing, that comes at odd times to the best of married men, with the best of wives and children – as Billy had. The other feeling, which came later on, and was a reaction in fact, was the feeling of a man who thinks he's been twisted round a woman's little finger for the benefit of somebody else. Billy said that be couldn't help being reminded by the shy, sweet smile and the shy, sweet "thank you" of the Pretty Girl in the Army, of the shy, sweet smile and the shy, sweet gratitude of a Sydney private barmaid, who had once roped him in, in the days before he was married. Then he'd reckon that the Army lassie had been sent out back to Bourke as a business speculation.

Tom Hall was inclined to reckon so too but that was after he'd been chaffed for a month about the three *War Crys*.

The Pretty Girl was discussed from psychological points of view; not forgetting the sex problem. Donald Macdonald – shearer, union leader and labour delegate to other colonies on occasion – Donald Macdonald said that whenever he saw a circle of plain or ugly, dried-up women or girls round a shepherd, evangelist or a Salvation Army drum, he'd say "sexually starved!" They were hungry for love. Religious mania was sexual passion dammed out of its course. Therefore he held that morbidly religious girls were the most easily seduced.

But this couldn't apply to Pretty Girl in the Army. Mitchell reckoned that she'd either had a great sorrow – a lot of trouble, or a disappointment in love (the "or" is Mitchell's); but they couldn't see how a girl like her could possibly be disappointed in love – unless the chap died or got into jail for life. Donald decided that her soul had been starved somehow.

Mitchell suggested that it might be only a craving for notoriety, the same thing that makes women and girls go amongst lepers, and out to the battlefield and nurse ugly pieces of men back to life again; the same thing that makes some women and girls swear ropes round men's necks. The Pretty Girl might be the daughter of well-to-do people even aristocrats, said Mitchell. She was pretty enough and spoke well enough. "'Every woman's a barmaid at heart,' as the Bulletin puts it," said Mitchell.

But not even one of the haggard women of Bourke ever breathed a suspicion of scandal against her. They said she was too good and too pretty to be where she was. You see it was not as in an old settled town where hags blacken God's world with their tongues. Bourke was just a little camping town in a big land, where free, good-hearted democratic Australians, and the best of black sheep from the old world were constantly passing through; where husbands were often obliged to be away from home for twelve months, and the storekeepers had to trust the people, and mates trusted each other, and the folks were broad-minded. The mind's eye had a wide range.

After her maiden speech the Pretty Girl seldom spoke, except to return thanks for collections – and she never testified. She had a sweet voice and used to sing.

Now, if I were writing pure fiction, and were not cursed with an obstinate inclination to write the truth, I might say that, after the advent of the Pretty Girl, the morals of Bourke improved suddenly and wonderfully. That One-eyed Bogan left off gambling and drinking and fighting and swearing, and put on a red coat and testified and fought the devil only; that Mitchell dropped his mask of cynicism; that Donald Macdonald ate no longer of the tree of knowledge and ceased to worry himself with psychological problems, and was happy; and that Tom Hall was no longer a scoffer. That no one sneaked round through the scrub after dusk to certain necessary establishments in weather-board cottages on the outskirts of the town; and that the broad-minded and obliging ladies thereof became Salvation Army lassies.

But none of these things happened. Drunks quieted down or got out of the way if they could when the Pretty Girl appeared on the scene, fights and games of "headin' 'em" were adjourned, and weak, ordinary language was used for the time being, and that was about all.

Nevertheless, most of the chaps were in love with that Pretty Girl in the Army – all those who didn't *worship* her privately. Long Bob Brothers hovered round in hopes, they said, that she'd meet with an accident – get run over by a horse or something – and he'd have to carry her in; he scared the women at the barracks by dropping firewood over the fence after dark. Barcoo-Rot, the meanest man in the back country, was seen to drop a threepenny bit into the ring, and a rumour was industriously circulated (by Tom Hall) to the effect that One-eyed Bogan intended to shave and join the Army disguised as a lassie.

Handsome Jake Boreham (alias Bore-'em), a sentimental shearer from New Zealand, who had read Bret Harte, made an elaborate attempt for the Pretty Girl, by pretending to be going to the dogs headlong, with an idea of first winning her sorrowful interest and sympathy, and then making an apparently Hard struggle to straighten up for Her sake. He related his experience with the cheerful and refreshing absence of reserve which was characteristic of him, and is of most bushmen.

"I'd had a few drinks," he said, "and was having a span under a gum by the river, when I saw the Pretty Girl and another Army woman coming down along the bank. It was a blazing hot day. I thought of Sandy and the Schoolmistress in Bret Harte, and I thought it would be a good idea to stretch out in the sun and pretend to be helpless; so I threw my hat on the ground and lay down, with my head in a blazing heat, in the most graceful position I could get at, and I tried to put a look of pained regret on my face, as if I was dreaming of my lost boyhood and me mother. I thought, perhaps, the Girl would pity me, and I felt sure she'd stoop and pick up my hat and put it gently over my poor troubled head. Then I was going to become conscious for a moment, and look hopelessly round, and into her eyes, and then start and look sorrowful and ashamed, and stagger to my feet, taking off my hat like the Silver King does to the audience when he makes his first appearance drunk on the stage; and then I was going to reel off, trying to walk as straight as I could. And next day I was going to clean up my teeth and nails and put on a white shirt, and start to be a new man henceforth.

"Well, as I lay there with my eyes shut, I heard the footsteps come up and stop, and heard 'em whisper, and I thought I heard the Pretty Girl say 'Poor fellow!' or something that sounded like that; and just then I got a God-almighty poke in the ribs with an umbrella – at least I suppose it was aimed for my ribs; but women are bad shots, and the point of the umbrella caught me in the side, just between the bottom rib and the hipbone, and I sat up with a click, like the blade of a pocket-knife.

"The other lassie was the big square-faced woman. The Pretty Girl looked rather more frightened and disgusted than sentimental, but she had plenty of pluck, and soon pulled herself together. She said I ought to be ashamed of myself, a great big man like me, lying there in the dust like a drunken tramp – an eyesore and a disgrace to all the world. She told me to go to my camp, wherever that was, and sleep myself sober. The square-jawed woman said I looked like a fool sitting there. I did feel ashamed, and I reckon I did look like a fool – a man generally does in a fix like that. I felt like one, anyway. I got up and walked away, and it hurt me so much that I went over to West Bourke and went to the dogs properly for a fortnight, and lost twenty quid on a game of draughts against a blindfold player. Now both those women had umbrellas, but I'm not sure to this day which of 'em it was that gave me the poke. It wouldn't have mattered much anyway. I haven't borrowed one of Bret Harte's books since.

Jake reflected a while.

"The worst of it was," he said ruefully, "that I wasn't sure that the girl or the woman didn't see through me, and that worried me a bit. You never can tell how much a woman suspects, and that's the worst of 'em. I found that out after I got married."

The Pretty Girl in the Army grew pale and thin and bigger-eyed. The women said it was a shame, and that she ought to be sent home to her friends, wherever they were. She was laid up for two or three days. and some of the women cooked delicacies and handed 'em over the barracks fence, and offered to come in and nurse her; but the square woman took washing home and nursed the girl herself.

The Pretty Girl still sold *War Crys* and took up collections, but in a tired, listless, half shamed-faced way. It was plain that she was tired of the Army, and growing ashamed of the Salvationists. Perhaps she had come to see things too plainly.

You see, the Army does no good out back in Australia – except from a business point of view. It is simply there to collect funds for hungry headquarters. The bushmen are much too intelligent for the Army. There was no poverty in Bourke as it is understood in the city; there was plenty of food; and camping out and roughing it come natural to the bushmen. In cases of sickness, accident, widows or orphans, the chaps sent round the hat, without banging a drum or testifying, and that was all right. If a chap was hard up he borrowed a couple of quid from his mate. If a strange family arrived without a penny, someone had to fix 'em up, and the storekeepers helped them till the man got work. For the rest, we work out our own salvation, or damnation – as the case is – in the bush, with no one to help us, except a mate, perhaps. The Army can't help us, but a fellowsinner can, sometimes, who has been through it all himself. The Army is only a drag on the progress of Democracy, because it attracts many who would otherwise be aggressive Democrats – and for other reasons.

Besides, if we all reformed the Army would get deuced little from us for its city mission.

The Pretty Girl went to service for a while with the stock inspector's wife, who could get nothing out of her about herself or her friends. She till slept at the barracks, stuck to the Army, and attended meetings.

It was Christmas morning, and there was peace in Bourke and goodwill towards all men. There hadn't been a fight since yesterday evening, and that had only been a friendly one, to settle an argument concerning the past ownership, and, at the same time, to decide as to the future possession of a dog.

It had been a hot, close night, and it ended in a suffocating sunrise. The free portion of the male population were in the habit of taking their blankets and sleeping out in "the Park," or town square, in hot weather; the wives and daughters of the town slept, or tried, to sleep with bedroom windows and doors open, while husbands lay outside on the verandas. I camped in a corner of the park that night, and the sun woke me.

As I sat up I caught sight of a swagman coming along the white, dusty road from the direction of the bridge, where the cleared road ran across west and on, a hundred and thirty miles, through the barren, broiling mulga scrubs, to Hungerford, on the border of Sheol. I knew that swagman's walk. It was John Merrick (Jack Moonlight), one-time Shearers' Union secretary at Coonamble, and generally "Rep." (shearers' representative), in any shed where he sheared. He was a "better-class shearer," one of those quiet, thoughtful men of whom there are generally two or three in the roughest of rough sheds, who have great influence, and give the shed a good name from a Union point of view. Not quiet with the resentful or snobbish reserve of the educated Englishman, but with a sad or subdued sort of quietness that has force in it – as if they fully realized that their intelligence is much higher than the average, that they have suffered more real trouble and heartbreak than the majority of their mates, and that their mates couldn't possibly understand them if they spoke as they felt and couldn't see things as they do yet men who understand and are intensely sympathetic in their loneliness and sensitive reserve.

I had worked in a shed with Jack Moonlight, and had met

him in Sydney, and to be mates with a bushman for a few weeks is to know him well – anyway, I found it so. He had taken a trip to Sydney the Christmas before last, and when he came back there was something wanting. He became more silent, he drank more, and sometimes alone, and took to smoking heavily. He dropped his mates, took little or no interest in Union matters, and travelled alone, and at night.

The Australian bushman is born with a mate who sticks to him through life – like a mole. They may be hundreds of miles apart sometimes, and separated for years, yet they are mates for life. A bushman may have many mates in his roving, but there is always one his mate, "my mate"; and it is common to hear a bushman, who is, in every way, a true mate to the man he happens to be travelling with, speak of *his* mate's mate – "Jack's mate" – who might be in Klondyke or South Africa. A bushman has always a mate to comfort him and argue with him, and work and tramp and drink with him, and lend him quids when he's hard up, and call him a b- fool and fight him sometimes; to abuse him to his face and defend his name behind his back; to bear false witness and perjure his soul for his sake; to lie to the girl for him if he's single, and to his wife if he's married; to secure a "pen" for him at a shed where he isn't on the spot, or, if the mate is away in New Zealand or South Africa, to write and tell him if it's any good coming over this way. And each would take the word of the other against all the world, and each believes that the other is the straightest chap that ever lived – "a white man!" And next best to your old mate is the man you're tramping, riding, working, or drinking with.

About the first thing the cook asks you when you come along to a shearers' hut is, "Where's your mate?" I travelled alone for a while one time, and it seemed to me sometimes, by the tone of the inquiry concerning the whereabouts of my mate, that the bush had an idea that I might have done away with him and that the thing ought to be looked into.

When a man drops mateship altogether and takes to "batting" in the bush, it's a step towards a convenient tree and a couple of saddle-straps buckled together.

I had an idea that I, in a measure, took the place of Jack Moonlight's mate about this time.

" 'Ullo, Jack!" I hailed as be reached the corner of the park. "Good morning, Harry!" said Jack, as if he'd seen me yesterday evening instead of three months ago. "How are you getting on?"

We walked together towards the Union Office, where I had a camp in the skillion-room at the back. Jack was silent. But there's no place in the world where a man's silence is respected so much (within reasonable bounds) as in the Australian bush, where every man bas a past more or less sad, and every man a ghost – perhaps from other lands that we know nothing of, and speaking in a foreign tongue. They say in the bush, "Oh, Jack's only thinking!" And they let him think. Generally you want to think as much as your mate; and when you've been together some time it's quite natural to travel all day without exchanging a word. In the morning Jim says, "Well, I think I made a bargain with that horse, Bill," and some time late in the afternoon., say twenty miles farther on, it occurs to Bill to "rejoin," "Well, I reckon the blank as sold it to you had yer proper!"

I like a good thinking mate, and I believe thinking in

company is a lot more healthy and more comfortable, as well as less risky, than thinking alone.

On the way to the Union Office Jack and I passed the Royal Hotel, and caught a glimpse, through the open door, of a bedroom off the veranda, of the landlord's fresh, fair, young Sydney girl-wife, sleeping prettily behind the mosquito-net, like a sleeping beauty, while the boss lay on a mattress outside on the veranda, across the open door. (He wasn't necessary for publication, but an evidence of good faith.)

I glanced at Jack for a grin, but didn't get one. He wore the pained expression of a man who is suddenly hit hard with the thought of something that might have been.

I boiled the billy and fried a pound of steak.

"Been travelling all night, Jack?" I asked.

"Yes," said Jack. "I camped at Emus yesterday."

He didn't eat. I began to reckon that he was brooding too much for his health. He was much thinner than when I saw him last, and pretty haggard, and he had something of the hopeless, haggard look that I'd seen in Tom Hall's eyes after the last big shearing strike, when Tom had worked day and night to hold his mates up all through the hard, bitter struggle, and the battle was lost.

"Look here, Jack!" I said at last. "What's up?"

"Nothing's up, Harry," said Jack. "What made you think so?"

"Have you got yourself into any fix?" I asked. "What's the Hungerford track been doing to you?"

"No, Harry," he said, "I'm all right. How are you?" And he pulled some string and papers and a roll of dusty pound notes from his pocket and threw them on the bunk.

I was hard up just then, so I took a note and the billy to go to the Royal and get some beer. I thought the beer might loosen his mind a bit.

"Better take a couple of quid," said Jack. "You look as if you want some new shirts and things." But a pound was enough for me, and I think he had reason to be glad of that later on, as it turned out.

"Anything new in Bourke?" asked Jack as we drank the beer.

"No," I said, "not a thing – except there's a pretty girl in the Salvation Army."

"And it's about time," growled Jack.

"Now, look here, Jack," I said presently, "what's come over you lately at all? I might be able to help you. It's not a bit of use telling me that there's nothing the matter. When a man takes to brooding and travelling alone it's a bad sign, and it will end in a leaning tree and a bit of clothesline as likely as not. Tell me what the trouble is. Tell us all about it. There's a ghost, isn't there?"

"Well, I suppose so," said Jack. "We've all got our ghosts for that matter. But never you mind, Harry; I'm all right. I don't go interfering with your ghosts, and I don't see what call you've got to come haunting mine. Why, it's as bad as kicking a man's dog." And he gave the ghost of a grin.

"Tell me, Jack," I said, "is it a woman?"

"Yes," said Jack, "it's a woman. Now, are you satisfied?"

"Is it a girl?" I asked.

"Yys," he said.

So there was no more to be said. I'd thought it might have been a lot worse than a girl. I'd thought he might have got married somewhere, sometime, and made a mess of it.

We had dinner at Billy Woods's place, and a sensible Christmas dinner it was – everything cold, except the vegetables, with the hose going on the veranda in spite of the by-laws, and Billy's wife and her sister, fresh and cool-looking and jolly, instead of being hot and brown and cross like most Australian women who roast themselves over a blazing fire in a hot kitchen on a broiling day, all the morning, to cook scalding plum pudding and redhot roasts, for no other reason than that their grandmothers used to cook hot Christmas dinners in England.

And in the afternoon we went for a row on the river, pulling easily up the anabranch and floating down with the stream under the shade of the river timber – instead of going to sleep and waking up helpless and soaked in perspiration, to find the women with headaches, as many do on Christmas Day in Australia.

Mrs Woods tried to draw Jack out, but it was no use, and in the evening he commenced drinking, and that made Billy uneasy. "I'm afraid Jack's on the wrong track," he said.

After tea most of us collected about Watty's veranda. Most things that happened in Bourke happened at Watty's pub, or near it.

If a horse bolted with a buggy or cart, he was generally stopped outside Watty's, which seemed to suggest, as Mitchell said, that most of the heroes drank at Watty's – also that the pluckiest men were found amongst the hardest drinkers. (But sometimes the horse fetched up against Watty's sign and lamp-post – which was a stout one of "iron-bark" – and smashed the trap.) Then Watty's was the

Carriers' Arms, a union pub; and Australian teamsters are mostly hard cases: while there was something in Watty's beer which made men argue fluently, and the best fights came off in his backyard. Watty's dogs were the most quarrelsome in town, and there was a dog-fight there every other evening, followed as often as not by a man-fight. If a bushman's horse ran away with him the chances were that he'd be thrown on to Watty's veranda, if he wasn't pitched into the bar; and victims of accidents, and sick, hard-up shearers, were generally carried to Watty's pub, as being the most convenient and comfortable for them. Mitchell denied that it was generosity or good nature on Watty's part, he said it was all business-advertisement. Watty knew what he was doing. He was very deep, was Watty. Mitchell further hinted that if he was sick he wouldn't be carried to Watty's, for Watty knew what a thirsty business a funeral was. Tom Hall reckoned that Watty bribed the Army on the quiet.

I was sitting on a stool along the veranda wall with Donald Macdonald, Bob Brothers (the Giraffe) and Mitchell, and one or two others, and Jack Moonlight sat on the floor with his back to the wall and his hat well down over his eyes. The Army came along at the usual time, but we didn't see the Pretty Girl at first – she was a bit late. Mitchell said he liked to be at Watty's when the Army prayed and the Pretty Girl was there; he had no objection to being prayed for by a girl like that, though he reckoned that nothing short of a real angel could save him now. He said his old grandmother used to pray for him every night of her life and three times on Sunday, with Christmas Day extra when Christmas Day didn't fall on a Sunday; but Mitchell reckoned that the old lady couldn't have had much influence because he became more sinful every year, and went deeper in ways of darkness, until finally he embarked on a career of crime.

The Army prayed, and then a thin "ratty" little woman bobbed up in the ring; she'd gone mad on religion as women do on woman's rights and hundreds of other things. She was so skinny in the face, her jaws so prominent, and her mouth so wide, that when she opened it to speak it was like a ventriloquist's dummy and you could almost see the cracks open down under her cars.

"They say I'm cracked!" she screamed in a shrill, cracked voice. "But I'm not cracked – I'm only cracked on the Lord Jesus Christ! That's all I'm cracked on –." And just then the Amen man of the Army – the Army groaner we called him, who was always putting both feet in it – just then he blundered forward, rolled up his eyes, threw his hands up and down as if he were bouncing two balls, and said, with deep feeling:

"Thank the Lord she's got a crack in the right place!"

Tom Hall doubled up, and most of the other sinners seemed to think there was something very funny about it. And the Army, too, seemed struck with an idea that there was something wrong somewhere, for they started a hymn.

A big American negro, who'd been a night watchman in Sydney, stepped into the ring and waved his arms and kept time, and as he got excited he moved his hands up and down rapidly, as if he was hauling down a rope in a great hurry through a pulley block above, and he kept saying, "Come down, Lord!" all through the hymn, like a bass accompaniment,

"Come down, Lord; come down, Lord; come down, Lord; come down, Lord!" and the quicker he said it the faster he hauled. He was as good as a drum. And, when the hymn was over, he started to testify.

"My frens!" he said, "I was once black as der coals in der mined! I was once black as der ink in der ocean of sin! But now – thank an' bless the Lord! – I am whiter dan der dribben snow!"

Tom Hall sat down on the edge of the veranda and leaned his head against a post and cried. He had contributed a bob this evening, and he was getting his money's worth.

Then the Pretty Girl arrived and was pushed forward into the ring. She looked thinner and whiter than I'd ever seen her, and there was a feverish brightness in her eyes that I didn't like.

"Men!" she said, "this is Christmas Day –" I didn't hear any more for, at the sound of her voice, Jack Moonlight jumped up as if he'd sat on a baby. He started forward, stared at her for a moment as if he couldn't believe His eyes, and then said, "Hannah!" short and sharp. She started as if she was shot, gave him a wild look, and stumbled forward; the next moment he had her in his arms and was steering for the private parlour.

I heard Mrs Bothways calling for water and smelling-salts; she was as fat as Watty, and very much like him in the face, but she was emotional and sympathetic. Then presently I heard, through the open window, the Pretty Girl say to Jack, "Oh, Jack, Jack! Why did you go away and leave me like that? It was cruel!"

"But you told me to go, Hannah," said Jack. "That – that

didn't make any difference. Why didn't you write?" she sobbed.

"Because you never wrote to me, Hannah," he said.

"That – that was no excuse!" she said. "It was so k-k-k-cruel of you, Jack."

Mrs Bothways pulled down the window. A new-comer asked Watty what the trouble was, and he said that the Army girl had only found her chap, her husband, or long-lost brother or something, but the missus was looking after the business; then he dozed again.

And then we adjourned to the Royal and took the Army with us.

"That's the way of it," said Donald Macdonald. "With a woman it's love or religion; with a man it's love or the devil."

"Or with a man," said Mitchell, presently, "it's love and the devil both, sometimes, Donald."

I looked at Mitchell hard, but for all his face expressed he might only have said, "I think it's going to rain."

SOLUTIONS TO BRAIN TEASERS

Page 10

1.			D	A	R	L	I	N	G	
2.	V	I	C	T	O	R	I	A		
3.			N	E	P	E	A	N		
4.				G	E	O	R	G	E	S
5.	F	I	T	Z	R	O	Y			

Page 16

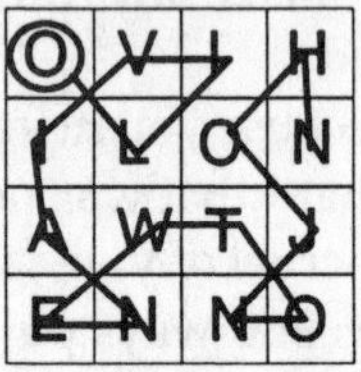

Page 21

Sport: 1. (b); 2. (c); 3. (a); 4. (c); 5. (c). 6. (c); 7. (b); 8. (d); 9. (c); 10. (d). 11. (a); 12. (d); 13. (c); 14. (b); 15. (d). 16. (b); 17. (a); 18. (b); 19. (d); 20. (c).

Page 41

Art/Entertain: 1. (b); 2. (d); 3. (c); 4. (c); 5. (b); 6. (b); 7. (c); 8. (d); 9. (b); 10. (a); 11. (a); 12. (a); 13. (b); 14. (d); 15. (c); 16. (c); 17. (a); 18. (c); 19. (b); 20. (b).

Page 22

F	L	I	P	S
C	L	I	P	S
C	H	I	P	S
C	H	I	N	S
C	O	I	N	S

Page 26

	1	2	3	4	5
1	N	O	O	S	A
2	O	P	A	L	S
3	O	A	S	I	S
4	S	L	I	C	E
5	A	S	S	E	T

Page 41

1.				R	O	M	A				
2.				B	R	O	O	M	E		
3.	B	A	L	L	A	R	A	T			
4.					R	E	N	M	A	R	K
5.				Z	E	E	H	A	N		

Page 58

1. COOLANGATTA
2. GUNDAGAI
3. WOLLONGONG
4. COLLINGWOOD
5. DANDENONG
6. ROCKHAMPTON
7. LAUNCESTON
8. KATHERINE

SOLUTIONS TO BRAIN TEASERS

Page 61

(Crossword solution)
1. PHARLAP
2. POSSUM
3. (MOOMBA)
4. ABMOOM / ASKIN
5. NOLAN
6. NAMATSIRA
7. (CILA)
8. EASTER / ECILA
9. ROSELLA

Page 64

KEEP NOT ILL MEN COMPANY LEST YOU INCREASE THE NUMBER.

Page 72

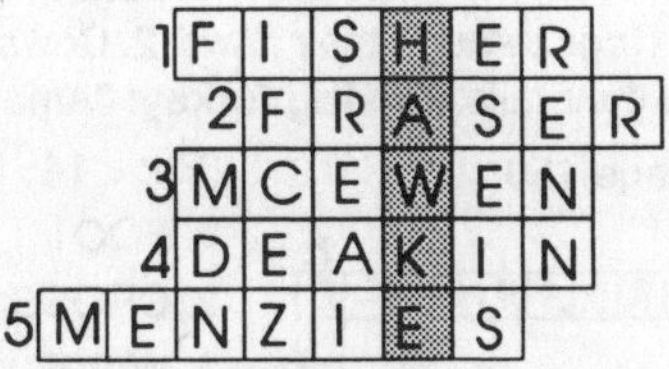

1. FISHER
2. FRASER
3. MCEWEN
4. DEAKIN
5. MENZIES

Page 82

A	¹FEARED	² FREED	³ DEER	F
N	⁴INSTEP	⁵ SPITE	⁶ PETS	I
D	⁷SADDLE	⁸ DEALS	⁹ LEAD	S
R	¹⁰REACH	¹¹ ACHE	¹² ACE	H
E	¹³PLEASE	¹⁴ LAPSE	¹⁵ PALS	E
W	¹⁶WRITE	¹⁷ TIER	¹⁸ TIE	R

Page 90

1. FLATHEAD
2. PERCH
3. COD
4. MULLET
5. WHITING

Page 94

1. KITTY; 2. STATE; 3. TEMPT; 4. TESTY; 5. ATTIC

Page 98

1. Greenland
2. Australia
3. Singapore
4. Swaziland

Page 89

The Past: 1. (c); 2. (c); 3. (b); 4. (d); 5. (b); 6. (c); 7. (b); 8. (c); 9. (c); 10. (a); 11 (c); 12. (b); 13. (a); 14. (c); 15. (b); 16. (b); 17. (b); 18. (b); 19. (a); 20. (d).

Page 138

Poem 1:

There was movement at the station, for the word had passed around

That the colt from Old Regret had got away

Poem 2:

I'd like to see green grass again

And watch clear water run

Away from this unholy plain

And flies, and dust, and sun.

SOLUTIONS TO BRAIN TEASERS

Pages 127-128

Phobias: Fear of ... 1.The Night; 2.Ridicule; 3. Being Stared At; 4.Thirteen; 5.Work; 6.Cats.**Animal cries:** 1. Bell; 2. Squeak; 3. Pipe or warble; 4. Drum; 5. Gibber; 6. Caw. **Are you being facetious:** The words are: "abstemious" and "facetious" **Spelling test:** The letter is "a" **Sweat on this:** 1. Dogs through their paws; 2. Cows through their noses; 3. Potaroos through their tails. **Talking turkey:** "American birds"

Page 150

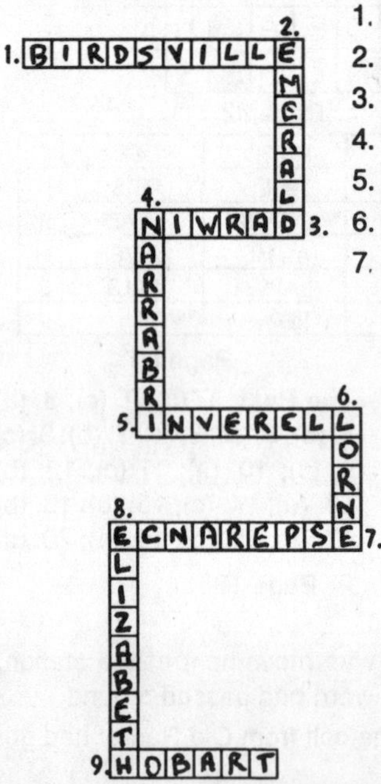

Page 145

1. FOOT
2. CROSS
3. WAVE
4. POUND
5. MOUTH
6. SPRING
7. LOUNGE

Page 160

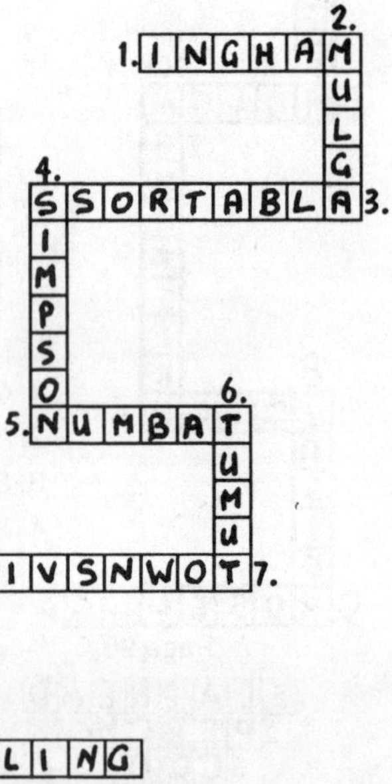

Page 156

HE WAS SHEARING WHEN I KNEW HIM, SO I SENT THE LETTER TO HIM

JUST ON SPEC, ADDRESSED AS FOLLOWS, "CLANCY, OF THE OVERFLOW"